D0568284

Student Achievement Goal Setting:

Using Data to Improve Teaching and Learning

James H. Stronge
Leslie W. Grant

EYE ON EDUCATION
6 DEPOT WAY WEST, SUITE 106
LARCHMONT, NY 10538
(914) 833–0551
(914) 833–0761 fax
www.eyeoneducation.com

Copyright © 2009 Eye On Education, Inc.
All Rights Reserved.

For information about permission to reproduce selections from this book, write:
Eye On Education, Permissions Dept., Suite 106, 6 Depot Way West,
Larchmont, NY 10538.

Library of Congress Cataloging-in-Publication Data

Stronge, James H.
Student achievement goal setting : using data to improve teaching and learning
/ James H. Stronge, Leslie W. Grant.
        p. cm.
    ISBN 978-1-59667-114-0
1. Educational tests and measurements--Data processing. 2. Academic achieve-
ment--Data processing. 3. School improvement programs--Data processing. I.
Grant, Leslie W. 1968- II. Title.
LB3051.S883 2008
371.26'0285--dc22

                                                    2008044573

10 9 8 7 6 5 4 3 2 1

Also Available from EYE ON EDUCATION

Handbook on Teacher Evaluation:
Assessing and Improving Performance
James H. Stronge and Pamela D. Tucker

Handbook on Educational Specialist Evaluation:
Assessing and Improving Performance
James H. Stronge and Pamela D. Tucker

People First: The School Leader's Guide
to Building & Cultivating Relationships with Teachers
Jennifer Hindman, Angela Seiders, and Leslie Grant

Handbook on Teacher Portfolios
for Evaluation and Professional Development
Pamela D. Tucker, James H. Stronge, and Christopher R. Gareis

Teacher-Made Assessments:
How to Connect Curriculum, Instruction, and Student Learning
Christopher R. Gareis and Leslie W. Grant

Data, Data Everywhere:
Bringing the Data All Together for Continuous School Improvement
Victoria L. Bernhardt

Data Analysis for Continuous School Improvement, 2nd Edition
Victoria L. Bernhardt

School Leader's Guide to Root Cause Analysis:
Using Data to Dissolve Problems
Paul G. Preuss

Using Data to Improve Student Learning Series
Elementary Schools
Middle Schools
High Schools
School Districts
Victoria L. Bernhardt

The School Portfolio Toolkit: A Planning, Implementation,
and Evaluation Guide for Continuous School Improvement
Victoria L. Bernhardt

Data-Driven Instructional Leadership
Rebecca J. Blink

Dedication

To all of the teachers who make a difference in the lives of their students and whose dedication and work result in greater student success.

Table of Contents

About the Authors

James H. Stronge, PhD is the Heritage Professor in the Educational Policy, Planning, and Leadership Area at the College of William and Mary, Williamsburg, Virginia. His research interests include policy and practice related to teacher quality, and teacher and administrator evaluation. His work on teacher quality focuses on how to identify effective teachers and how to enhance teacher effectiveness. Dr. Stronge has presented his research at numerous national and international conferences such as the American Educational Research Association, the University Council for Educational Administration, the National Evaluation Institute, the Association for Supervision and Curriculum Development; and the European Council of International Schools. Additionally, he has worked extensively with local school districts on issues related to teacher quality, teacher selection, and teacher and administrator evaluation.

Stronge has authored, coauthored, or edited 20 books and more than 90 articles, chapters, and technical reports. His recent books include the following:

- *Qualities of Effective Principals* (Association for Supervision and Curriculum Development, 2008)

- *Qualities of Effective Teaching*, 2nd ed. (Association for Supervision and Curriculum Development, 2007)

- *The Teacher Quality Index: A Protocol for Teacher Selection* (Association for Supervision and Curriculum Development, 2006)

- *Linking Teacher Evaluation and Student Achievement* (Association for Supervision and Curriculum Development, 2005)

- *Evaluating Teaching*, 2nd ed. (Corwin Press, 2005)

- *Handbook for Qualities of Effective Teachers* (Association for Supervision and Curriculum Development, 2004)

Dr. Stronge has been a teacher, counselor, and district-level administrator. His doctorate is in the area of Educational Administration and Planning from the University of Alabama. He may be contacted at: The College of William and Mary, School of Education, P.O. Box 8795, Williamsburg, VA 23187-8795, 757-221-2339, or jhstro@wm.edu.

Leslie W. Grant, PhD, is a Visiting Assistant Professor in the Curriculum and Instruction and Educational Leadership areas at the College of William and Mary in Williamsburg, Virginia. Dr. Grant is the coauthor of *Teacher-Made Assessments: How to Connect Curriculum, Instruction, and Student Learning*, and she is the contributing author to *Qualities of Effective Teachers* (2nd ed.) written by James Stronge. She has worked with school districts in the areas of teacher evaluation, student achievement goal setting, and student assessment. Dr. Grant has presented her work at national conferences such as the Association for Supervision and Curriculum Development, the National Association of Elementary School Principals, the National Staff Development Council, and the National Title I Conference. She was a teacher and instructional leader before serving as a developer of state customized assessments for a major test publishing company. Her doctorate degree is in Educational Policy, Planning, and Leadership from the College of William and Mary. Dr. Grant can be contacted at: The College of William and Mary, School of Education, P.O. Box 8795, Williamsburg, VA 23187-8795, lwgran@wm.edu.

Acknowledgments

The creation of a project is never an isolated endeavor. This was certainly true in the development of this book. To move from imagination to culmination required the encouragement, support, and assistance of many individuals. We take this opportunity to acknowledge the contributions of many friends, generous colleagues, and capable students.

Colleagues from both universities and school districts with which we have worked contributed to the development of the practices described in the book as well as the refinement of the text itself. In particular, Pamela Tucker, University of Virginia, and Chris Gareis, the College of William and Mary, offered conceptual and technical support for this project. Additionally, Jennifer Hindman, the College of William and Mary, provided invaluable assistance and encouragement for our student achievement goal setting work, particularly in our efforts to field test the goal setting processes with selected schools and school districts.

We appreciate numerous external reviewers for their thoughtful reviews and insightful comments for improving the text. Mary Vause, a graduate student at the College of William and Mary, also assisted this effort through her careful review and editing of the manuscript prior to publication. Finally, we are particularly indebted to Bob Sickles for his faith in us to develop a new Eye On Education book series, *Research to Practice,* that focuses on the heart of education, which is teaching and learning. *Student Achievement Goal Setting: Using Data to Improve Teaching and Learning* is the first book in this series. We trust that you will find it beneficial to your practice as you continue to promote the success of your students.

Thank you,
JHS and LWG

Preface

Introduction

Can we boost student achievement through improved teacher work? Can we document student growth over time and thus improve student learning? In *Student Achievement Goal Setting: Using Data to Improve Teaching and Learning*, we focus on improving student achievement through academic goal setting—a process in which teachers:

- Determine benchmark performance for the students.
- Set achievement goals based on where the students begin.
- Monitor progress throughout the academic year or other learning period.
- Measure performance at the end of the year.

Thus, student achievement goal setting provides a fair, realistic, and feasible method to implement instruction to increase student achievement in any school or classroom.

In advocating student achievement goal setting, we do not mean the traditional professional goals in which teachers or other educators set "personal growth" goals. By all means, we encourage educators to continue their growth, but we focus on growth that is defined and aimed explicitly at improved student performance. If the goal (or any school-based activity, for that matter) doesn't improve or contribute to the quality of life of a child, we probably shouldn't be investing our scarce resources in it. For us, the phrase "student achievement goal setting" means focusing instruction, assessment, professional development, and, in fact, the full array of teacher endeavors on improving student achievement. By achievement, we don't necessarily mean an end-of-year benchmark state test. Although this is one measure of student (and teacher) success, we are more interested in making student achievement goal setting applicable to the broad range of what students should know and be able to do. After all, this is what our job as educators is all about.

Finally, we want to emphasize that our goal in this goal-setting book is not to bring you one more personal theory or idea on how to instruct students or improve student learning. It seems we have enough untested theories, ideas, and methods already. Instead, what we need as a profession is to inform our teaching and learning experiences with the most applicable research available, and that is our intent in *Student Achievement Goal Setting: Using Data to Improve Teaching and Learning.* Although we don't believe that this new text is the definitive answer to improved teaching and learning, we do hope we are able to provide you, our reader, with a solid plank in the bridge connecting research and good practice.

How the Book Is Organized

The book is organized into three sections:

♦ Part I provides a conceptual framework and explains how to implement student achievement goal setting.

♦ Part II offers numerous sample goals, cutting across various grade levels and subject areas as well as professional positions.

♦ Part III includes an annotated bibliography of key publications that are related to the concepts and practice of student achievement goal setting.

Chapter 1 of Part I explains how goal setting for student achievement works and also provides empirical research to support the practice. In Chapter 2 we move to a thorough review and explanation, accompanied by numerous examples of how goal setting really works when it is focused on improving student performance. Chapter 3 adds insight and practice-based guidance for how to assess students in goal setting. In Chapter 4, we offer guidance to consider before, during, and after implementation of student achievement goal setting.

Part II of the book provides examples both of student achievement goals set by teachers and of student achievement and/or program goals set by educational specialists such as guidance counselors, library or media specialists, and a host of others who impact students through their work. A chart is provided that details the position of the professional, the school level, and the subject or program area addressed by the goal. The reader is free to find an example that best suits his or her educational position.

Part III of the book provides an annotated bibliography of selected publications, along with a matrix that relates the publications to various aspects of student achievement goal setting. Our intent is to offer a user-friendly source for those who want to explore the concepts and research underlying student achievement goal setting.

Uses for the Book

Student achievement goal setting focuses on the value that teachers and educational specialists add to the learning process and to educational programs. *Student Achievement Goal Setting: Using Data to Improve Teaching and Learning* equips educational professionals with the necessary tools and with a plan of action so that they can use student achievement data to improve instructional practice and increase student achievement. The book can be a valuable resource for the following audiences:

- Teachers, including classroom teachers, resource teachers, and teachers in other settings, who desire to improve their own teaching and their students' learning;

- Educational specialists who support student learning through administration of educational programs and who know the value they bring to the educational process;

- Teacher leaders who are in a position to positively impact teacher practice through their support and expertise;

- Administrators who supervise and support teachers; and

- Staff development specialists who plan and deliver training focused on improving instructional practices.

It is our sincere hope that *Student Achievement Goal Setting: Using Data to Improve Teaching and Learning* benefits your school, your teaching practices, and, most importantly, your students.

Part I

How Student Achievement Data Can Be Used to Improve Student Learning

1

What Is Student Achievement Goal Setting?

Introduction

Why do we have schools? Other than safety, we can identify only two reasons why schooling exists as an enterprise:

Reason 1: Teaching and learning

Reason 2: Supporting teaching and learning

The only justification for public (or private, for that matter) education to exist is to improve the quality of life of our students, and the primary way we do this is by helping them learn to read, to understand math, to appreciate the world around them, to be prepared to productively participate in their world, to live healthy and happy lives, and so forth. In other words, everything we do in education—everything—should positively touch the life of a child.

In *Student Achievement Goal Setting: Using Data to Improve Teaching and Learning* we focus on the ultimate goal of education—improved student achievement. In this introductory chapter, we summarize the research supporting student achievement goal setting in the classroom and discuss how teachers set appropriate goals based on relevant data. More specifically, in this opening chapter we discuss the following questions related to student achievement goal setting:

♦ What is it?

♦ How does it work?

♦ Why use it?

♦ What does the research say about it?

3

♦ How does it relate to formative assessment?

We address each of these key questions in turn.

Student Achievement Goal Setting: What Is It?

Related Definitions

Assessment for Learning:

"Assessment for learning is any assessment for which the first priority in its design and practice is to serve the purpose of promoting students' learning. It thus differs from assessment designed primarily to serve the purposes of accountability, or of ranking, or of certifying competence."[2]

Curriculum-Based Measurement:

A term used in special education circles in which student needs are assessed in terms of what they should be able to learn and be able to do, teachers set goals in the individualized education plan (IEP) based on perceived gaps, and then teachers continually monitor student progress and make adjustments as needed.[3]

Progress Monitoring:

"First, teachers determine the students' current levels of performance… Second, teachers use the students' current levels of performance to establish ambitious but realistic achievement goals…Third, teachers determine the rate of progress."[4]

We reiterate that student achievement goal setting exists for two reasons: improving student learning and supporting teachers in their work with students. We will discuss the former throughout the book, but the latter deserves explanation. One approach to linking student achievement to teacher performance involves building the capacity for teachers and their supervisors to interpret and use student achievement data to set target goals for student improvement. Indeed, school districts across the United States and other countries have incorporated student achievement goal setting as one measure of student progress.[1] Setting goals—not just any goals, but goals focused squarely on student performance—is a powerful way to enhance professional performance and, in turn, positively impact student achievement.

Student achievement goal setting is sometimes described as "student progress monitoring." Student progress monitoring has been described as a process in which:

> …the teacher determines a student's current performance level on skills that the student will be learning that school year, identifies achievement goals that the student needs to reach by the end of the year, and establishes the rate of progress the student must make to meet those goals. The teacher then measures the student's academic progress regularly (weekly, biweekly, or monthly) using probes, which are brief and easily administered measures.[5]

These steps provide a succinct definition of student achievement goal setting.

How Does Student Achievement Goal Setting Work?

In practical terms, the student achievement goal-setting process can be depicted in the following five steps (Figure 1.1).

Figure 1.1. Student Achievement Goal-Setting Process

- ◆ Step 1: What is the starting point for student learning (i.e., documenting where students begin their learning)?

- ◆ Step 2: What reasonable, but measurable, goals should they be expected to achieve, given where they start?

- ◆ Step 3: What specific teaching strategies should be used with specific students?

- ◆ Step 4: Where are the students in terms of achieving their desired learning goals throughout the instructional period? What mid-point corrective action should be taken to enhance student learning (i.e., what adjustments to instruction can be made to enhance learning)?

- ◆ Step 5: Where are students at the end of the year/term/unit of instruction?

Student achievement goal setting begins with knowing where students are in relation to what is expected of them. This allows teachers to set specific, measurable goals based on both the demands of the curriculum and the needs of the students. The next part of the process is recursive in that the teacher creates and implements strategies and monitors the progress of those strategies. As progress is monitored, the teacher makes adjustments to the teaching and learning strategies. Finally, a summative judgment is made regarding student learning for a specified period of time. The process looks similar to Figure 1.2.

Figure 1.2

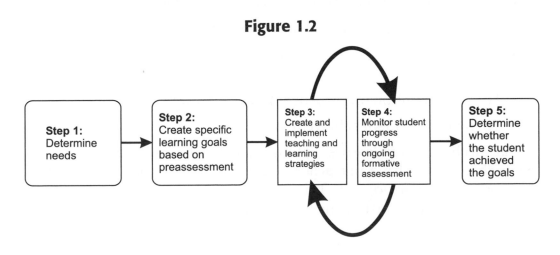

Special Education: A Special Case for Goal Setting

Special education instruction can be considered a special kind of student goal setting. For special education students, the U.S. Individuals with Disabilities Education Act (IDEA) requires an integration between assessment and instruction. Additionally, IDEA mandates that each IEP include a statement of measurable annual goals, including academic and functional goals designed to meet the child's individual needs.[6] Additionally, IDEA requires a description of how the child's progress toward meeting these goals will be measured.[7] In essence, special educators are required to deliver differentiated instruction that is specified in IEPs and which includes procedures for assessing student progress toward goals.[8] According to Fuchs and colleagues, this goal-setting process is defined by frequent curriculum-based measurement and evaluation.[9]

Although full-blown IEPs for all students may not be feasible, nonetheless, it is a close hybrid that we advocate for all students—a process in which we know where our students begin, what we can do to help them maximize their learning, whether our instructional strategies are succeeding, and, most importantly, how well our students have actually learned. This is student achievement goal setting.

Why Student Achievement Goal Setting?

We know that teachers have a definite and powerful impact on student learning and academic performance.[10] In this vein, student achievement goal setting allows teachers to focus attention on students and on instructional improvement through the process of determining baseline performance, developing strategies for improvement, and assessing results at the end of the academic year. More specifically, the intent of student achievement goal setting is the following:

♦ To make explicit the connection between teaching and learning,

♦ To make instructional decisions based on student data,

♦ To provide a tool for school improvement,

♦ To increase effectiveness of instruction through continuous professional growth,

♦ To focus attention on student results, and, ultimately,

♦ To increase student achievement.[11]

That all children can learn is "an implicit belief that most teachers share, and it is a belief that should drive all teachers' efforts in the classroom with each and every child, each and every day."[12] This is precisely the reason that we advocate for setting rigorous yet realistic achievement goals for all students. We should not only believe that all children can learn but also *expect* all students to learn, and we should create a structure for them through which learning can occur.

The Power of Student Achievement Goal Setting: What Does the Research Say?

Goal setting based on student achievement data is supported by solid research in the field (see, for example, Cawelti, 2004; Marzano, Pickering, & Pollock, 2001; Snipes, Doolittle, & Herlihy, 2002; Walberg, 1984).[13] Good and Brophy stated in their summary of effective classroom practices that "setting goals and making a commitment to trying to reach these goals increases performance."[14] They found that goal setting is particularly effective under the following conditions:

♦ The goals are proximal rather than distal (goals are oriented to the here-and-now rather than to some ultimate goal for the distant future, although it is important to make students conscious of the connection between here-and-now tasks and the accomplishment of ultimate goals).

♦ The goals are specific (but not too specific) rather than global.

♦ The goals are challenging (difficult but reachable rather than too easy or too hard).[15]

A number of well-established instructional strategies have been found to yield significantly improved student learning, and these strategies offer methods that closely parallel the student achievement goal-setting process, including methods that are related to direct impact on student learning and others that are related to school improvement.

Goal Setting: Impact on Student Learning

Goal Setting and Increased Student Achievement

Marzano, Pickering, and Pollock, in their work on research-based strategies for increasing student achievement, analyzed studies that showed percentile gains when using student goal setting ranging from 18 to 41.[16] Additionally, they drew the following three generalizations from the research on goal setting:

♦ Instructional goals narrow what students focus on. This means that although students generally score higher on the information related to a specific academic goal, they usually score lower—by approximately 8 percentile points—on information that is incidental to the goal but still covered in the class.

♦ Instructional goals should not be too specific. In other words, instructional goals stated in behavioral objective format do not produce student learning gains as high as instructional goals stated in more general formats.

♦ Students should be encouraged to personalize the teacher's goals. Once classroom academic goals are set, students should be encouraged to customize those goals to fit their personal needs.[17]

In discussing why educators should bother with target goals at all, one researcher stated that the best reason for implementing a goal-setting process is simply that it works.[18] In particular, researchers found that goal setting functions best when:

♦ Interventions are used that impact directly on the experience of learners.

♦ Ongoing reviews and feedback on student progress are associated with remedial actions.

♦ There are high teacher expectations of students.

♦ Formative assessment is emphasized.[19]

Despite the potential benefits of student achievement goal setting, there are possible negative consequences for students and teachers, and these are summarized in Figure 1.3.

Figure 1.3. Cautions about Student Achievement Goal Setting[20]

Possible Negative Consequences for Students	Possible Negative Consequences for Teachers
Goal setting could pose a threat to underachievers. If they are given low target goals, the students may underperform to their teachers' low expectations.	Individual goal setting may not be practical or cost effective.
Goals imply a narrowing of the many and varied purposes of education. This could result in a narrowing of important student learning opportunities.	The outcomes of learning are influenced by many external factors that cannot be controlled.
	Teachers are at risk of being blamed and being treated as scapegoats when their students do not meet goals.

Goal Setting and Progress Monitoring

Progress monitoring, which was described earlier in the chapter, is closely related to our description of student achievement goal setting. In a review of scientific research on progress monitoring, Fuchs and Fuchs summarized studies that produced very promising findings. Overall, they found that systematic progress monitoring can be used for the following purposes:

- To identify students in need of additional or different forms of instruction,
- To enhance instructional decision making by assessing the adequacy of student progress,
- To determine when instructional modifications are necessary,
- To prompt teachers to build stronger instructional programs that are more varied and responsive to students' personal needs.

The ultimate result of progress monitoring is better student achievement.[21]

In a study of teachers' use of accelerated math and continuous progress monitoring, the researchers found that students whose teachers used continuous progress monitoring significantly outperformed the students in control conditions.[22] Finally, in a review of continuous progress monitoring, the authors found that although progress-monitoring data alone did not appear to affect achievement, students realized significant gains when teachers responded to the continuous progress monitoring database by tailoring the instructional program to student needs.[23] In other words, teachers not only must be able to use and interpret data to monitor student progress, but also they must use the data to modify instruction. Suppose you are driving in your car and you glance at the fuel gauge. You notice that you have a quarter tank of gas. You continually monitor the gas gauge, but you never stop to get gas, even as it dips below the empty mark. Finally, the car stops running. Doesn't that behavior sound silly? That's what happens when we collect data regarding student achievement but do not use it. The negative outcome that results is the same as if we had not bothered to monitor at all.

Mastery Learning

Goal setting for student achievement is closely linked to mastery learning practices, also known as feedback-corrective teaching. It involves the following steps:

- Give students formative tests for the purposes of feedback.
- Provide corrective instructional procedures.

♦ Administer additional formative tests to determine the extent to which students have mastered the subject content.[24]

> **Mastery Learning**
>
> In practical terms, if students taught with traditional classroom instruction score at the 50th percentile on an assessment, students taught using mastery learning (a process very similar to student achievement goal setting) would be expected to score at the 84th percentile.[27]

In their seminal work, Black and Wiliam offered solid evidence that formative assessment is an essential component of classroom work and that it can raise student achievement.[25] Additionally, researchers such as Benjamin Bloom have found that students taught under mastery learning achieve, on average, 1.0 standard deviation above the average of students in conventional classrooms.[26]

Prerequisite Skills Assessment

Student achievement goal setting also is linked to enhancing students' initial cognitive entry prerequisites. This involves the following steps:

♦ Develop an initial skills assessment of prerequisites for a course or a unit of study.

♦ Administer the assessment to students at the beginning of a course.

♦ Teach students specific prerequisites that they lack.

Research indicates that on average, students who are taught prerequisite skills achieve approximately seven-tenths of a standard deviation above the average of students in conventionally taught classrooms (i.e., 76th percentile vs. 50th percentile).[28] This is a dramatic increase in student learning potential simply by assessing—and addressing—students' performance on important prerequisite skills *prior* to launching into the full curriculum.

To illustrate, a third- or fourth-grade student would be assessed on how well he or she understands multiplication *before* being taught long division. Why? Because it isn't feasible to teach students long division if they have not mastered the prerequisite of multiplication. Doing so would frustrate the student and would be futile for the teacher. Figure 1.4 provides two additional illustrations of how prerequisite skills work.

Figure 1.4. Prerequisite Cognitive Skills Examples

Content Area	What is the prerequisite?	Why assess for the prerequisite?
World language: Spanish II	Key skills that should have been attained in Spanish I	If a student doesn't understand the fundamental structure of the Spanish language (e.g., sound pronunciations, conjugation of regular verbs, commonly used nouns), he or she certainly won't understand more complex applications of reading, writing, listening, and speaking the language.
World geography	Key skills from multiple disciplines, including social sciences, mathematics, and reading	If a student cannot read a simple grid, then he or she won't be able to read and interpret maps, which is an essential skill in geography. If a student has no concept of what a country is, then he or she will not be able to engage at the level expected in high school world geography.

Any subject that is developmental in nature simply can't be successfully taught without addressing the basic knowledge and skills that are necessary to learn the content knowledge and more advanced skills of the course. Most of what we teach in pre-K–12 education is, by its very nature, developmental. Indeed, the developmental nature of subjects is evident in a spiral curriculum, an idea developed and refined in the 1960s through the work of Jerome Bruner and Hilda Taba, in which each year builds and expands on the knowledge and skills taught the previous year.[29]

Goal Setting: Impact on School Success

Standards-Based Learning

There is evidence that students in schools and school systems that implement a standards-based approach to performance assessment benefit from improved academic achievement. For example, the Thompson School District of Loveland, Colorado, implemented a standards-based performance system in which student learning was assessed as a component of teacher success. After two years of implementation, fourth-grade students in the district had the third-highest learning growth rank among Colorado's 176 school districts in reading as measured on the Colorado State Assessment Program (CSAP), and they had the highest growth rank in writing. Seventh graders experienced similar academic growth.[30]

Goal Setting and Data-Informed Decisions

Research revealed that school districts' use of data to make decisions and to set goals for school improvement leads to better student outcomes.[31] Studies of high-performing school districts found that these districts encourage teachers, schools, and the district as a whole to make decisions based on student achievement or progress data. They also train teachers on how to use assessments to guide instruction.[32]

In a study of five school districts that showed improvement for at least three years in mathematics and reading for all subgroups of students as identified by *No Child Left Behind*, researchers found that these five high-performing urban school districts focused on (1) using data to make instructional decisions and (2) training principals and teachers in how to use assessments for learning.[33] In a synthesis of research, it was found that high-performing school districts focus on making decisions based on data not only at the district level but also at the classroom and school levels as well.[34]

Goal Setting and Program Progress

Programs planned, implemented, and supported by teachers, instructional support professionals, and student services professionals impact overall student progress. Although program progress and student progress can be tied to teachers through student achievement data, the work of instructional support and student services professionals also contributes to student achievement and program goals. Consider the following research:

♦ High-quality libraries impact student achievement. Researchers found that schools with high-quality libraries have test scores that are 10 to 18 percent higher than schools with low-quality libraries, even when controlling for socioeconomic status. A high quality media specialist was a central component to a high quality library.[35]

♦ Studies of the impact of counselors on student achievement found that school counseling services make a difference in the academic performance of students. In three Florida counties, school counselors used targeted intervention with students. In these three counties where targeted interventions were used, students increased an average of 20 percentile points on the math section of the Florida Comprehensive Assessment Test (FCAT) and 15 percentile points on the reading FCAT.[36]

Formative Assessment: A Critical Component of Student Achievement Goal Setting

The focus on formative assessment in recent years has changed how we view the purposes and uses of assessment in the classroom.[37] Instead of using assessment merely to provide a summary judgment of student performance, assessment is now being seen as a vehicle *for* learning. Instruction and assessment are viewed as integral to each other *rather than* as separate activities that occur at separate points in the classroom.[38]

Popham defined formative assessment as "… a planned process in which assessment-elicited evidence of students' status is used by teachers to adjust their ongoing instructional procedures or by students to adjust their current learning tactics."[39] Furthermore, he stated that "… formative assessment is a potentially transformative instructional tool that, if clearly understood and adroitly employed, can benefit both educators and their students."[40] The power of formative assessment is its ability to inform instruction as instruction unfolds. Consider the following description of formative uses of student assessment:

An assessment activity can help learning if it provides information that teachers and their students can use as feedback in assessing themselves and one another and in modifying the teaching and learning activities in which they are engaged. Such assessment becomes "formative assessment" when the evidence is actually used to adapt the teaching work to meet learning needs.[41]

Michael Scriven was perhaps the first writer to apply the concepts of formative (ongoing, improvement-oriented) and summative (end-of-period, accountability-oriented) evaluation to education.[42] Subsequently, the formative-summative paradigm has been adopted broadly by the educational community and applied to varied settings, including student assessment.

What we advocate with student achievement goal setting is formative assessment in conjunction with summative assessment. Pre- and continuous assessment gives teachers the opportunity to determine where their students are *prior to* and *during* instruction while they can still impact learning outcomes. Although summative assessment plays an important role as well, if teachers wait until the end of the instructional unit to assess their students, they will merely be grading their students, not changing what they learn. Symbolically speaking, we contend that testing on Friday without first testing on Monday is wasted effort and lost opportunity.

Why Formative Assessment?

In formative assessment, instruction and assessment are inseparable aspects of teaching. Tomlinson noted in a discussion of the power of differentiated instruction for responding to the needs of all learners that one of the principles that guides differentiated classrooms is that assessment and instruction are inseparable. Furthermore, "in a differentiated classroom, assessment is ongoing and diagnostic."[43] Within the context of formative assessment and instructional differentiation, the effective teacher does the following:

- Recognizes the connection between instruction and assessment and uses daily classroom activities to assess and monitor student learning;

- Identifies student strengths and weaknesses and pinpoints where students are now and where they need to be;

- Focuses on strategies to close the gap between where the students are now and where they need to be;

- Provides feedback to students on their progress, both in terms of daily activities and overall progress; and

- Helps students learn how to assess themselves and provide constructive feedback to peers using established criteria for the task. [44]

These points build the foundation for steps 3 and 4 as shown in Figure 1.2. Looking back at the figure, one is reminded that just as formative assessment is a recursive process, so is this portion of student achievement goal setting. It is here that the dynamic between teacher and student becomes critical, and it is here where actual learning occurs. The other steps are essentially bookends to the process.

Researchers such as Black and Wiliam as well as Bloom indicated that formative assessment and the use of goal setting models such as mastery learning raise academic achievement.[45] Furthermore, students benefit academically in individual schools and in school districts where teachers are trained to use assessment data to guide instruction.[46]

Guskey described several ways to use classroom assessments to improve student learning.[47] In particular, teacher-administered assessments such as quizzes, tests, performance assessments, and writing prompts are good ways to target areas of improvement for student learning. Additionally, well designed assessments enhance the intended learning outcomes by offering immediate results. Guskey suggested three ways to use assessment for the improvement of student learning:

- ♦ Make assessments useful by relating the assessment to the concepts and skills discussed in class.[48] Then, students know what to study and can be rewarded for their learning, and teachers can perform item analyses on test items.

- ♦ Follow assessments with corrective instruction in which the teacher approaches the objectives with alternative strategies.[49] Students learn more, and the practice becomes a routine that does not require as much class time.

- ♦ Give second chances to demonstrate success so that assessments are not endpoints but are, instead, opportunities to acknowledge mastery and focus on areas of improvement.[50]

Why Not Standardized Tests Alone?

Standardized tests such as state accountability tests fulfill a fundamental purpose in education. That purpose is to evaluate school programs and target areas for improvement. However, they are less beneficial for identifying specific student needs within each discipline. They may indicate pockets of concern, but they are certainly unable to diagnose specific strengths and weaknesses.[51] Look at any state's test blueprint and you will find that a small number of questions are developed to provide evidence of learning across a very large number of curricular aims. That is an important reason why standardized tests, alone, should not be used in student achievement goal setting. Robert Stake expressed concern for how standardized tests are used in schools:

> Given continuous grading by teachers and almost continuous standardized testing, we do have pretty good measures of student performance on a large selection of academic tasks. But the tasks merely rank the students and tell us who the higher-performing ones are; they don't tell how educated they are.[52]

He further noted that we need a different type of student assessment if we are to understand student success and failure, and if we are to do something about it. Stake recommended focusing more energy and expertise on formative assessment: "This means putting more investment in ipsative (person-referenced) assessment and giving less credence to normative (norm-referenced) assessment."[53]

Summary

Data-driven decision-making permeates the education profession. By systematically examining data and establishing goals, educators—both teachers and administrators—can close the loop among multiple facets of their vocation, from the planning process all the way to assessment. Student achievement goal setting increases student learning by connecting assessment to the actions that occur in the learning environment, providing for far more seamless learning. Once we have established a learning goal based on students' performance in the beginning and where they must end up, we strategize how to help students get there with what we know works. Thus, assessment is the foundation for goal setting, and feedback for students and teacher is critical. In its most simplistic terms, student achievement goal setting is characterized by a set of interlocking steps:

- Where are students in the beginning?
- Where do we want them to be in the end?
- How do we get them to where they need to be?
- How are they doing along the way?
- And, finally, where are they in the end?

We provide a detailed discussion and review of the process of student achievement goal setting in Chapter 2.

1   Examples of school districts that use student achievement goal setting as part of their overall evaluation system at the time of the publication of this book include the following: Miami-Dade County Public Schools, Miami, Florida; Bedford County Public Schools, Bedford, Virginia; Greenville County Public Schools, Greenville, South Carolina.

2   Black, P., Harrison, C., Lee, C., Marshall, B., & Wiliam, D. (2004). Working inside the black box: Assessment for learning in the classroom. *Phi Delta Kappan, 86*(1), 9–21. p. 10.

3   Fuchs, L. S., Deno, S. L., & Mirkin, P. K. (1984). The effects of frequent curriculum-based measurement and evaluation on pedagogy, student achievement, and student awareness of learning. *American Educational Research Journal, 21*(2), 449–460.

4   Margolis, H. (2007). Monitoring your child's IEP: A focus on reading. *Insights on Learning Disabilities, 4*(2), 1–25. p. 3.

5   Safer, N., & Fleischman, S. (2005). Research matters: How student progress monitoring improves instruction. *Educational Leadership, 62*(5), 81–83. p. 81.

6   Individuals with Disabilities Education Act. 20 U.S.C. §1401 et seq., 34 C.F.R. §300.320. (2004).

7   Margolis, H. (2007).

8   Fuchs, L. S., Deno, S. L., & Mirkin, P. K. (1984).

9   Fuchs, L. S., Deno, S. L., & Mirkin, P. K. (1984).

10 See, for example, Tucker, P. D., & Stronge, J. H. (2005). *Linking student learning to teacher evaluation.* Alexandria, VA: Association for Supervision and Curriculum Development.

11 Tucker, P. D., & Stronge, J. H. (2005).

12 Gareis, C. R., & Grant, L. W. (2008). *Teacher-made assessments: How to connect curriculum, instruction, and student learning.* Larchmont, NY: Eye On Education.

13 Cawelti, G. (Ed.). (2004). *Handbook of research on improving student achievement* (2nd ed.). Arlington, VA: Educational Research Service.
    Marzano, R. J., Pickering, D. J., & Pollock, J. E. (2001). *Classroom instruction that works: Research-based strategies for increasing student achievement.* Alexandria, VA: Association for Supervision and Curriculum Development.
    Snipes, J., Doolittle, F., and Herlihy, C. (2002). *Foundations for success: Case studies of how urban school systems improve student achievement.* Washington, DC: Council of the Great City Schools.
    Walberg, H. J. (1984). Improving the productivity of America's schools. *Educational Leadership, 41*(8), 19–27.

14 Good, T. L., & Brophy, J. E. (1997). *Looking in classrooms* (7th ed.). NY: Addison-Wesley, p. 217.

15 Good, T. L., & Brophy, J. E. (1997).

16 Marzano, R. J., Pickering, D. J., & Pollock, J. E. (2001).

17 Marzano, R. J., Pickering, D. J., & Pollock, J. E. (2001). pp. 94-95.

18 Martinez, P. (2001). *Great expectations: Setting targets for students*. London: Learning and Skills Development Agency.

19 Martinez, P. (2001).

20 Martinez, P. (2001).

21 Fuchs, L. S., & Fuchs, D. (2003). *What is scientifically-based research on progress monitoring?* Washington, DC: National Center on Student Progress Monitoring.

22 Yesseldyke, J., & Bolt, D. M. (2007). Effect of technology-enhanced continuous progress monitoring on math achievement. *School Psychology Review, 36*(3), 453–467.

23 Stecker, P. M., Fuchs, L. S., & Fuchs, D. (2005). Using curriculum-based measurement to improve student achievement: Review of research. *Psychology in the Schools, 42*(8), 795–819.

24 Bloom, B. S. (1984). The search for methods of group instruction as effective as one-to-one tutoring. *Educational Leadership, 41*(8), 4–17.

25 Black, P., & Wiliam, D. (1998). Inside the black box: Raising standards through classroom assessment. *Phi Delta Kappan, 80*(2), 139–148.

26 Bloom, B. S. (1984).

27 Bloom, B. S. (1984).

28 Walberg, H. J. (1984).

29 Ornstein, A. C., & Hunkins, F. P. (1998). *Curriculum: Foundations, principles, and issues* (3rd ed.). Boston: Allyn and Bacon.

30 Stronge, J. H., & Tucker, P. D. (2000). *Teacher evaluation and student achievement*. Washington, DC: National Education Association.

31 Cawelti, G. (2004).

32 Snipes, J., Doolittle, F., & Herlihy, C. (2002).
    Togneri, W., & Anderson, W. E. (2003). *Beyond islands of excellence: What districts can do to improve instruction and achievement in all schools*. Alexandria, VA: Learning Alliance First.

33 Snipes, J., Doolittle, F., & Herlihy, C. (2002).

34 Cawelti, G. (2004).

35 Lance, K. C. (2004). Libraries and student achievement: The importance of school libraries for improving student achievement. *Threshold*, 8–9. Retrieved May 1, 2008, from http://www.ciconline.org.

36 Webb, L. D., Brigman, G. A., Campbell, C. (2005). Linking school counselors and student success: A replication of the student success skills approach to targeting the academic and social competence of students. *Professional School Counseling, 8*(5), 407–413.

37 Hargreaves, E. (2005). Assessment for learning? Thinking outside the (black) box. *Cambridge Journal of Education, 35*(2), 213–224.

38 Gareis, C. R., & Grant, L. W. (2008).

39 Popham, W. J. (2008). *Transformative assessment.* Alexandria, VA: Association for Supervision and Curriculum Development. p. 6.

40 Popham, W. J. (2008). p. 3.

41 Black, P., Harrison, C., Lee, C., Marshall, B., & Wiliam, D. (2004).

42 Scriven, M. S. (1967). The methodology of evaluation. In R. Tyler, R. Gagne, & M. Scriven (Eds.), *AERA monograph review on curriculum evaluation: No. 1* (pp. 39-83). Chicago: Rand McNally.

43 Tomlinson, C. A. (1999). *The differentiated classroom: Responding to the needs of all learners.* Alexandria, VA: Association for Supervision and Curriculum Development. p. 10.

44 Covino, E. A., & Iwanicki, E. (1996). Experienced teachers: Their constructs on effective teaching. *Journal of Personnel Evaluation in Education, 10*(4), 325–363.
Noonan, B., & Duncan, C. R. (2005). Peer and self-assessment in high schools. *Practical Assessment, Research, and Evaluation, 10*(17), 1–8.
Wharton-McDonald, R., Pressley, M., & Hampston, J. M. (1998). Literacy instruction in nine first-grade classrooms: Teacher characteristics and student achievement. *The Elementary School Journal, 99*(2), 101–128.

45 Black, P., & Wiliam, D. (1998); Bloom, B. S. (1984).

46 Snipes, J., Doolittle, F., & Herlihy, C. (2002); Tucker, P. D., & Stronge, J. H. (2005).

47 Guskey, T. R. (2003). How classroom assessments improve learning. *Educational Leadership, 60*(5), 6–11.

48 Guskey, T. R. (2003). p. 7.

49 Guskey, T. R. (2003). p. 9.

50 Guskey, T. R. (2003). p. 10.

51 Gareis, C. R., & Grant, L. W. (2008).

52 Stake, R. (1999). The goods on American education. *Phi Delta Kappan, 80*(9), 668–672. p. 668.

53 Stake, R. (1999). p. 672.

2

How to Design Student Achievement Goals

Introduction

In this chapter, we explain how to implement student achievement goal setting. We begin by providing an explanation and discussion of the systematic process involved in designing student achievement goals. In this "how to" chapter, we offer both poor examples and positive examples of student achievement goal setting through each step of the process. In an effort to help readers better understand the process of goal setting for student achievement, we address the following questions:

- What are the components of student achievement goal setting?
- How is the student achievement goal-setting process documented?
- How can a decision tree help the student achievement goal-setting process?

What Are the Components of Student Achievement Goal Setting?

In Chapter 1 we provided a general framework of student achievement goal setting. Essentially, the process involves five major steps:

- Step 1: Determine needs
- Step 2: Create specific learning goals based on needs
- Step 3: Create and implement teaching and learning strategies
- Step 4: Monitor student progress through ongoing formative assessment, and adjust as needed

♦ Step 5: Determine whether the student achieved the goals

You may recall from Chapter 1 that steps 3 and 4 are cyclical and can change throughout the goal-setting process to meet student needs. To exemplify all five steps we will examine two middle school language arts teachers who are moving through the goal-setting process. Teacher A misses the mark on each step and provides a poor example of how to implement the step. Teacher B understands each step and serves as a better example.

Step 1: Determine Needs

Any good teacher will tell you that he or she teaches both subject matter and students. Ignoring either the curriculum or specific learning needs ultimately hurts students' chances of success. If students are not exposed to the appropriate content at the appropriate cognitive level, then they might lack the knowledge and skills that are necessary for academic success. Conversely, if students' needs are ignored, then they might not be taught in a way that helps them to learn.

Curriculum Needs

Across the country, the move toward accountability means that state governments expect students to know certain content and have certain skills. In fact, as of 2008 all 50 states had adopted curriculum standards in the four core content areas: reading/language arts, mathematics, science, and social studies.[1] Many states, such as Virginia and Florida,[2] also have adopted standards in additional content areas, including visual arts, performing arts, foreign language, physical education, health, and driver education. School districts in most states further delineate the state's standards by developing district curriculum guidelines and pacing guides. Therefore, it is incumbent on teachers to ensure that their classroom achievement goals align with what the state expects students to know and be able to do.

Both schools and students are being held accountable for achieving state curriculum standards, underscoring how essential it is that goals focus on curriculum needs. As of 2008, 26 states rated schools based on student performance on state assessments, and 32 states sanctioned low-performing schools.[3] Students are being held accountable as well. For example, as of 2008 an eighth-grade student in the state of Georgia must pass the eighth-grade reading and math state assessments to be promoted to the ninth grade.[4] Starting in 2009, some states such as Maryland require that students pass tests to graduate.[5] Consequently, high stakes testing affects both educators and students. However, we should focus on state curriculum standards not only to pass tests—although that is an important reason—but also to gain the knowledge and skills necessary to be successful at the next academic level and eventually beyond K–12 education.

Student Needs

Although the state expects students to gain certain knowledge and skills, it is in the classroom that differences in students' performances become evident. In student achievement goal setting, goals are based on where students begin and where they should end. In an achievement-oriented society, many times we focus on the latter (i.e., the end result only), rather than on both the starting and ending points. Without knowing where students begin, an end-result measure alone is virtually useless because "we cannot even determine whether the students' achievement improved over time."[6]

Student achievement goal setting focuses on the gains that students make during the school year. Predictably, the cumulative effect of prior knowledge either sets students up to be successful or poses great challenges year to year. This prior knowledge and understanding must be taken into account.

Assessing student needs places goals in context and provides direction. The following contextual information may be helpful when formulating goals:

- ◆ *School information* such as the number of students, the free and reduced lunch rates, and the type of school such as rural, urban, or suburban; and

- ◆ *Student information* such as the number of students receiving special education services, the number of limited English proficiency students, and the number of students who are identified as gifted.

Contextual or preassessment information is important because it provides direction for the goal. For example, a ninth-grade teacher whose students lack fundamental skills to perform well in Algebra I will have very different achievement goals than a teacher who teaches Algebra I to seventh-grade students who have demonstrated a high level of proficiency in the fundamental skills. This is not to say that the first teacher has lower expectations of his or her students. He or she merely has a different starting point to move students toward success.

Another key reason to consider contextual information in setting achievement goals is to create realistic goals and, thus, give the teacher and students opportunities to see the goals achieved. For example, if the ninth-grade Algebra I teacher noted above has a number of students with specific learning disabilities (SLD) or numerous English as a second language (ESL) learners in his class, then the achievement goals for those students likely would be different from those for students without disabilities or for native English speakers.

Figure 2.1 offers examples of issues to consider in setting individual, subgroup, and classroom achievement goals.

Figure 2.1. Step 1: Determine Student Needs

	Context or Special Considerations for Setting Goals	Preassessment Information for Students
Teacher A: Poor example	I will focus my goal on the two tenth-grade English classes that I teach. There are a total of 54 students in the two classes.	Last year my students performed poorly on the state writing exam. We will work on writing this year.
Teacher B: Better example	I teach two classes of tenth-grade English in an urban high school of approximately 2,500 students. Forty-four percent of the students in the school receive free and reduced lunch. I have a total of 57 students in the two classes. Twenty-nine percent of my students have IEPs and qualify for special education services. Specifically, eight of the 57 have been diagnosed with dysgraphia, a severe problem with handwriting.	For the past three years, my students have had inconsistent performance on the state writing examination. I administered writing prompts for both expository writing and persuasive writing to my students in early September and scored the students' work using the state writing rubric. The data showed that 28% of my students scored 4 points (proficiency level) or better on the expository writing sample, and 20% of my students scored 4 points or better on the persuasive writing sample.

Teacher A provides minimal information regarding the students and the school, and he gives inadequate preassessment data about the students' initial knowledge and skills. It may be that Teacher A does not know his students' learning needs and, therefore, cannot accommodate them. Additionally, the information provided fails to give adequate context. Are the majority of students gifted or in need of special services? Teacher A also fails to base his goal on preassessment data of the students he teaches. The data to which he refers is from last year's group of students, not this year's.

Teacher B, conversely, provides useful contextual information, such as background information about the school and about the students in his classroom. He has knowledge of the significant and individualized needs of his students and can use this information to develop appropriate student learning goals. He also has solid assessment data on which to base his goal. Teacher B refers to the state writing assessment to note a three-year, downward trend in writing performance. However, he doesn't stop with state assessment data. To confirm that writing is an issue with the current students, he administers a preassessment in which students respond to both an expository writing prompt and a persuasive writing prompt. He uses the state writing rubric to score the responses, thus attending to both curriculum needs and student needs. Teacher B now has a starting point and can create an appropriate achievement goal. Figure 2.2 provides the baseline data for the class.

Figure 2.2. Baseline Data for Expository and Persuasive Essay for Teacher B.*

	Number and Percent of Students Earning Each Score Point on the Essays						
	Unscorable	1	2	3	4	5	6
Expository: Baseline	3 (5%)	7 (12%)	12 (21%)	19 (33%)	8 (14%)	5 (9%)	3 (5%)
Persuasive: Baseline	2 (3%)	9 (16%)	14 (25%)	21 (37%)	5 (9%)	4 (7%)	2 (3%)

*Percentages do not equal 100 as a result of rounding.

Step 2: Create Specific Learning Goals Based on Preassessment Data

This step is the linchpin of student achievement goal setting, and it provides the basis for the other steps. The first consideration is to ensure that the goal is based on relevant student achievement data. Without a starting point it would be difficult to look ahead to the end of the school year. In goal setting, understanding where students start is paramount to

Numerous research studies have examined factors that correlate with student achievement. These related factors are addressed in Step 1 of the goal-setting process and include:

- A challenging curriculum[7] —To achieve, students must be exposed to a full, rigorous curriculum. This means that students are taking the courses they need to be successful, and the courses focus on meaningful content.

(continues...)

- Student mobility[8]—Students who change schools frequently are more likely to be below grade level than their peers who attend the same school over a longer period of time. Factors such as student mobility can help place a student learning goal in context.

- Prior achievement[9]—By examining standardized test data, a teacher can have an idea of the prior achievement of students in his or her class. This does not mean, however, that the teacher has lower expectations. Rather, the teacher has an idea of the relative strengths and weaknesses of his or her students. In fact, in one study examining prior achievement and the impact of a teacher, both factors had a comparable impact on student achievement.[10]

- Diagnosis and corrective action[11]—Diagnosing where students are reveals specific areas of strengths and weaknesses. Corrective action, which comes during instruction, makes use of diagnostic information to plan for student needs.

successful implementation. There are, however, additional important considerations.

A goal must be meaningful. A goal that is too broad may be difficult to track and measure. A goal that lacks a time frame may become lost and forgotten. Goals should be concrete, specific, and trackable.[12] Additionally, goals should be set high, but not so high that the teacher views the goal as out of reach. An individual may not put forth much effort on easy goals and may throw up his or her hands in despair with goals that are seen as unachievable. Rather, a good achievement goal—one that is both worthy and attainable—is a stretch goal. The ideal goal satisfies the Goldilocks analysis: It's not too high, not too low, but just right.

To assist in the development of meaningful goals, we use the "SMART" criteria as shown below (Figure 2.3).

Figure 2.3. SMART Criteria

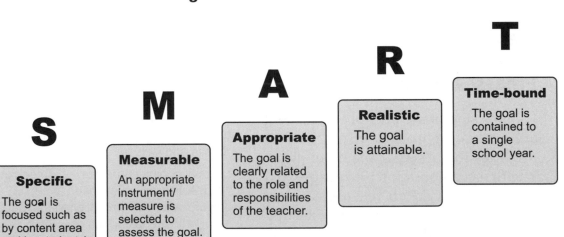

Specific
The goal is focused such as by content area and by students' needs.

Measurable
An appropriate instrument/ measure is selected to assess the goal.

Appropriate
The goal is clearly related to the role and responsibilities of the teacher.

Realistic
The goal is attainable.

Time-bound
The goal is contained to a single school year.

- *Specific:* First, goals should be specific. What content is addressed in the goal? Without this information, it would be difficult to measure and track progress.

- *Measurable:* The second criterion is that the goal is measurable and uses an appropriate instrument. For example, Teacher A in Figure 2.2 uses state writing results for last year's students as the basis for his goal. This is an inappropriate use of assessment data and will lead to a goal that is not meaningful for the teacher or the students. Teacher B, however, uses a relevant measurement (current students' writing prompts scored with the state writing rubric).

- *Appropriate:* The third criterion is appropriateness. A goal that is appropriate is directly related to the subject and students that the teacher teaches or the program that the educational specialist administers. A teacher who teaches mathematics will have more of a direct effect on students' mathematics achievement rather than on the students' science achievement, although elements of mathematics are certainly present in science.

- *Realistic:* If a goal is to be attainable, it must also be realistic. A realistic goal does not mean an easy goal, which would be meaningless. A realistic goal should stretch the outer bounds of what is attainable.

- *Time-bound:* Finally, the goal should be time-bound. A distal goal can be hard to track and can become lost over time, whereas a goal bound by time will be definitive and allow for determining if, in fact, the goal has been achieved. Generally, we recommend setting student achievement goals for one school year or one semester if the school is on a block schedule, thus providing a definite beginning and end.

Figure 2.4 shows the goals developed by both Teachers A and B. As you review the goals, consider whether they satisfy the SMART criteria.

A review of studies on goal setting found the following conclusions, among others:[13]

- A majority of the studies reviewed showed that when a goal was more difficult, performance improved. The researchers concluded that when difficult goals are established, people tend to work harder.

- Specific, quantifiable goals led to higher performance than vague goals such as "students will improve" or "I will do my best" or no goals at all. However, specific goals can cause individuals to focus on the goal area to the exclusion of other areas of need.

**Figure 2.4. Step 2: Create Specific Learning Goals
Based on Needs Assessment**

	Student Achievement Goal
Teacher A: Poor example	The students will improve in their writing ability.
Teacher B: Better example	For the current school year, all of my students will make measurable progress on both expository writing and persuasive writing by improving by at least one performance level as measured by the state writing rubric. In other words, by the end of the school year, 61% of my students will score 4 points (proficiency) or better out of a possible 6 on the expository writing sample and 56% of my students will score 4 points or better on the persuasive writing sample.

Teacher A's goal misses the mark on many of the SMART criteria. It lacks specificity and an appropriate measurement, and it provides no indication of the time involved. The goal itself, however, is appropriate as the instructor does teach English, and it is quite realistic in that many students will improve in writing. Teacher B, conversely, provides a goal that meets the SMART criteria. At the end of the year, Teacher B will be able to determine whether he has met his goal.

Step 3: Create and Implement Teaching and Learning Strategies

Strategies—that is, the actual "how to"—are the link between goal context and goal attainment. Strategies are how learning and student improvement happen. Therefore, strategies should be chosen carefully and should have the following characteristics:

♦ Supported by research

♦ Developmentally appropriate

♦ Appropriate for the subject matter

A great deal of literature and numerous studies examine effective teaching strategies.[14] Although effective strategies are central to goal setting, we do not seek to provide a list of these strategies by developmental appropriateness and by subject matter. Rather, we encourage teachers to examine their teaching practices and read education research to provide the most effective instruction to students. Figure 2.5 illustrates the strategies identified by Teacher A and Teacher B.

**Figure 2.5. Step 3: Create and Implement
Teaching and Learning Strategies**

	Instructional Strategies
Teacher A: Poor example	I will work with my students to improve their writing skills by sending home grammar and/or mechanics drills and then checking homework on a regular basis. Students also will write weekly themes.
Teacher B: Better example	I will employ the following strategies to address student needs: Use frequent formative assessments in skill-specific areas related to writing expository and persuasive essays, and provide feedback to students. Use Writer's Workshop, teaching mini-lessons on specific areas related to writing essays, including composition, written expression, mechanics, and usage. Complete a three-day workshop on teaching writing to adolescents.

Teacher A provides a general idea of strategies he will use. Unfortunately, these are too broad and general to be of value in differentiating instruction for the particular learning needs of his students. Significantly, these ineffective strategies focus only on what the students will do rather than what the teacher will do with student work. We know the students will be writing weekly themes, but we are not sure what Teacher A will be doing with the student work. Teacher B, however, provides very specific strategies that are appropriate to both the students and the subject area. Frequent formative assessments result in increased student achievement.[15] Writer's Workshop increases student literacy skills and focuses on analyzing student strengths and weaknesses, as well as adjusting for both.[16] Coursework is also associated with increased teacher effectiveness.[17] In short, Teacher B's strategies are specific and supported by research and experts in the field.

Step 4: Monitor Student Progress

Chapter 1 provided an overview of the student achievement goal-setting process. Figure 2.6 below is identical to Figure 1.2 from Chapter 1, and it shows the interconnectedness between steps 3 and 4. The relationship is cyclical in that student progress is monitored, and adjustments are made on a daily, weekly, or year-long basis. In the goal-setting process we focus on a formal review of goal progress at mid-year, but monitoring of student progress is most beneficial under the following conditions: when it is done on a frequent basis, when progress is monitored on discrete sets of knowledge and skills, and when that progress is shared and examined with students. However, monitoring alone is not enough. Instruction must be adjusted based on the information gleaned from frequent classroom assessments. As Stiggins explained, "When they assess for learning, teachers use the classroom assessment process and the continuous flow of information about student achievement that it provides in order to advance, not merely check on, student learning."[18]

Figure 2.6.

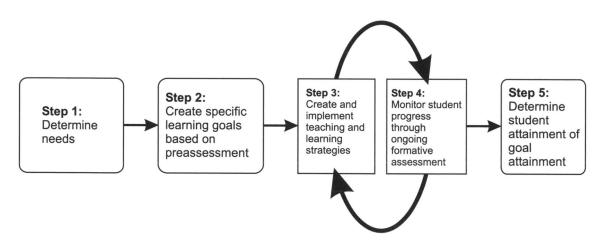

As stated, we advocate for a more formal mid-year or mid-term review in which teachers share progress toward the goal in a collegial venue. The benefits of a specific mid-year review are numerous. Teachers can take stock and make changes to overall strategies as needed, and they can also talk with each other to gain support and ideas to improve student learning. However, challenges can exist as well. These include creating an atmosphere in which teachers are comfortable sharing this information and providing time for them to do it. Additionally, teachers need guidance in how to structure the review so that it will provide focus.[19]

Figure 2.7 provides the mid-year review by Teacher A and Teacher B. Notice that both teachers indicate that students are improving. However, Teacher B provides more specific information to show that students are indeed improving. In Figure 2.8, he illustrates the improvement by showing the percentages of students scoring at each performance level. Teacher B also adds another strategy that he learned in his writing workshop and decides to incorporate it into his overall strategy to improve student writing. He plans to use the state writing rubric to teach students self- and peer-assessment.

Figure 2.7. Step 4: Monitor Student Progress and Adjust

	Mid-Year Progress Review
Teacher A: Poor Example	At mid-year the students seem to be making progress based on my review of their weekly themes. I will continue to work with each student to address individual student needs.
Teacher B: Better Example	I administered the expository and persuasive writing samples to my students. They are showing improvement in their writing. I have seen an increase from 28 percent to 32 percent of students scoring a four or higher on the expository essay and an increase from 20 percent to 30 percent of students scoring four or higher on the persuasive essay. I will continue with my strategies and work to differentiate instruction and assessments for student needs. Additionally, I am going to begin to work with students on assessing their own writing and each other's writing according to the state writing rubric.

**Figure 2.8. Number and Percent of Students
Scoring at Performance Levels at Mid-Year for Teacher B.***

	Number and Percent of Students Earning Each Score Point on the Essays						
	Unscorable	1	2	3	4	5	6
Expository: Baseline	3 (5%)	7 (12%)	12 (21%)	19 (33%)	8 (14%)	5 (9%)	3 (5%)
Expository: Mid-year	2 (4%)	4 (7%)	11 (19%)	22 (39%)	10 (18%)	6 (11%)	2 (3%)
Persuasive: Baseline	2 (3%)	9 (16%)	14 25%)	21 (37%)	5 (9%)	4 (7%)	2 (3%)
Persuasive: Mid-year	1 (2%)	2 (4%)	18 (32%)	19 (33%)	8 (14%)	6 (11%)	3 (5%)

*Percentages do not equal 100 as a result of rounding.

Step 5: Determine Student Achievement of Goals

The final part of the process is determining whether students have improved and whether the teacher has met the learning goal that he or she established. Determining the achievement of the goals is directly related to the quality of the goal created. If the goal is, indeed, "SMART" then evaluating goal attainment will be straightforward. Figure 2.9 illustrates how Teacher A and Teacher B documented goal attainment. Notice that with Teacher A we are not sure how many students improved, and how much they improved. Teacher B's response indicates that the goal was met, and Figure 2.10 provides data for support. Teacher B relates the goal attainment directly back to the goal itself.

Figure 2.9. Step 5: Determine Student Achievement of Goals

	Evidence of Goal Attainment
Teacher A: Poor example	Overall, the students improved in their writing prompts.
Teacher B: Better example	Based on the writing prompts administered in May of the current year, 63% of my students scored 4 points or better on the expository writing sample and 57% of my students scored 4 points or better on the persuasive writing sample. All of my students improved in their writing scores. The attached chart illustrates how the students improved.

Figure 2.10. End-of-Year Data Results from Teacher B*

	Number and Percent of Students Earning Each Score Point on the Essays						
	Unscorable	1	2	3	4	5	6
Expository: Baseline	3 (5%)	7 (12%)	12 (21%)	19 (33%)	8 (14%)	5 (9%)	3 (5%)
Expository: End of Year*	0 (0%)	3 (5%)	7 (12%)	11 (19%)	20 (35%)	8 (14%)	8 (14%)
Persuasive: Baseline	2 (3%)	9 (16%)	14 (25%)	21 (37%)	5 (9%)	4 (7%)	2 (3%)
Persuasive: End of Year*	0 (0%)	2 (4%)	9 (16%)	14 (25%)	20 (35%)	6 (11%)	6 (11%)

*Percentages do not equal 100 as a result of rounding.

Putting It All Together: How Is the Student Achievement Goal-Setting Process Documented?

Teachers set daily, weekly, quarterly, and year-long goals for their students, and they often use anecdotal evidence or observations to provide an indication of whether students are meeting goals. However, we recommend documenting the goal-setting process to move beyond anecdotes toward empirical evidence of student growth. Many teachers find that documenting the process is quite rewarding because they actually see on paper that they have made a difference in what students have learned. Documenting the process also professionalizes the work that teachers do. The teachers collect and analyze data and then set goals based on those data. Student achievement goal setting is predicated on the professional knowledge and skills that teachers possess. The goal is created by the teacher rather than imposed by an outside influence. This critical element makes the goal specific to the teacher and encourages ownership of the goal.

The Student Achievement Goal-Setting Form

A template for documenting the process is provided in Figure 2.11. Notice how each section corresponds to the five steps discussed in this chapter. Figure 2.12 shows how the sections on the form correspond to the five steps.

Figure 2.11. Student Achievement Goal-Setting Form

Teacher's Name:_____	
School:_____ Position:_____ School Year:____–____	
I. Setting (Describe the population and special learning circumstances.)	
II. Content/Subject/Field Area (The area/topic addressed based on learner achievement, data analysis, or observational data)	
III. Baseline Data (What does the current data show?)	
IV. Goal Statement (Describe what you want students to accomplish.)	
V. Strategies (Activities used to accomplish the goal)	
VI. Mid-Year Review (Describe goal progress and other relevant data.)	
VII. End-of-Year Results (Accomplishments at the end of the year)	

**Figure 2.12. Correspondence of Student Achievement
Goal-Setting Steps to Sections on the Goal-Setting Form**

Student Achievement Goal-Setting Steps	Student Achievement Goal-Setting Form Sections
Step 1—Determine needs.	Section I—Setting Section II—Content/Subject/Field Area Section III—Baseline Data
Step 2—Create student achievement goals based on needs.	Section IV—Goal Statement
Step 3—Create and implement teaching and learning strategies.	Section V—Strategies
Step 4—Monitor student progress and make adjustments, if necessary.	Section VI—Mid-Year review
Step 5—Determine goal attainment.	Section VII—End-of-year results

Examples of Documenting Student Achievement Goal Setting

In this chapter we followed two teachers as they moved through the student achievement goal-setting process. Figure 2.13 shows Teacher A's complete form, and Figure 2.14 shows Teacher B's completed form.

Figure 2.13. Teacher A—Student Achievement Goal-Setting Form (Poor Example)

Teacher's Name: <u>Teacher A</u>	
School: <u>School A</u> Position: <u>Eighth-Grade English Teacher</u>	

I. Setting (Describe the population and special learning circumstances.)	I will focus my goal on the two tenth-grade English classes that I teach. There are a total of 54 students in the two classes.
II. Content/Subject/Field Area (The area/topic addressed based on learner achievement, data analysis, or observational data)	Writing, based on the state standards and state writing rubric
III. Baseline Data (What does the current data show?)	Last year my students performed poorly on the state writing exam.
IV. Goal Statement (Describe what you want students to accomplish.)	The students will improve in their writing ability.
V. Strategies (Activities used to accomplish the goal)	I will work with my students to improve their writing skills by sending home grammar/mechanics drills and then checking homework on a regular basis. Students also will write weekly themes.
VI. Mid-Year Review (Describe goal progress and other relevant data.)	At mid-year the students seem to be making progress based on my review of their weekly themes. I will continue to work with each student to address individual student needs.
VII. End-of-Year Data Results (Accomplishments at the end of the year)	Overall, the students improved in their writing prompts.

Figure 2.14. Teacher B—Student Achievement
Goal-Setting Form (Better Example)

Teacher's Name: Teacher B	
School: School B Position: Eighth-Grade English Teacher	
I. Setting (Describe the population and special learning circumstances.)	I teach two classes of tenth-grade English students in an urban high school of approximately 2,500 students. Forty-four percent of the students in the school receive free and reduced lunch. I have a total of 57 students in the two classes. Twenty-nine percent of my students qualify for special education services and have IEPs. Specifically, 8 of the 57 have dysgraphia, a severe problem with handwriting.
II. Content/ Subject Area (The area/topic addressed based on learner achievement, data analysis, or observational data)	Writing
III. Baseline Data (What does the current data show?)	For the past three years, my students have had inconsistent performance on the state writing examination. I administered writing prompts for both expository writing and persuasive writing to my students in early September and scored the students' work using the state writing rubric. The data show that 28% of my students scored 4 points (proficiency level) or better on the expository writing sample, and 20% of my students scored 4 points or better on the persuasive writing sample.

continued

IV. Goal Statement (Describe what you want students to accomplish.)	For the current school year, all of my students will make measurable progress on both expository writing and persuasive writing by improving by at least one performance level as measured by the state writing rubric. In other words, by the end of the school year, 61% of my students will score 4 points (proficiency) or better out of a possible 6 points on the expository writing sample, and 56% of my students will score 4 points or better on the persuasive writing sample.
V. Strategies (Activities used to accomplish the goal)	I will employ the following strategies to address student needs: • Use frequent formative assessments in skill-specific areas related to writing expository and persuasive essays, and provide feedback to students. • Use Writer's Workshop, teaching mini-lessons on specific areas related to writing essays, including composition, written expression, mechanics, and usage. • Complete a three-day workshop on effective strategies to teach writing to adolescents.
VI. Mid-Year Review (Describe goal progress and other relevant data.)	I administered the expository and persuasive writing samples to my students. They are showing improvement in their writing. I have seen an increase from 28 percent to 32 percent of students scoring a four or higher on the expository essay and an increase from 20 percent to 30 percent of students scoring four or higher on the persuasive essay. I will continue with my strategies and work to differentiate instruction and assessments for student needs. Additionally, I am going to begin to work with students on assessing their own writing and on assessing each other's writing according to the state writing rubric.

continued

VII. End-of-Year Data Results (Accomplishments at the end of the year)	Based on the writing prompts administered in May of the current year, 63% of my students scored 4 points or better on the expository writing sample, and 57% of my students scored 4 points or better on the persuasive writing sample. All of my students improved in their writing scores. The attached graph illustrates how the students improved.

We previously analyzed each individual part of the goal-setting process, and now we will analyze the process holistically. Comparison of the two forms reveals the following:

- Both teachers focus on writing, an area under their specific purview.

- Both teachers document the entire process on the form.

- Teacher A's form is quite general, whereas Teacher B's form is specific and provides details and data for support.

- Teacher A's form is vague, and we are not certain of the nature and degree of progress that students made. Teacher B's form provides a clear picture of where students were in the beginning of the year in writing and where they were at the end of the year. Therefore, we see a legitimate gain in student progress.

It is clear from viewing the forms that Teacher B systematically used the goal-setting process to improve student learning. This conclusion cannot be drawn about Teacher A. Although Teacher A may have used the process systematically, we cannot adequately ascertain student achievement growth by reviewing the form. The process is easier to follow and more useful when the documentation is specific and practical.

Specifying the Student Achievement Goal-Setting Process

The language used in the student achievement goal-setting process can help to provide a clearer and stronger connection between teaching processes and student learning. This chapter has focused on providing examples of teacher goals; however, educational specialists such as library/media specialists, guidance counselors, school psychologists, school social workers, and school nurses also can be included in the process of performance goal setting. Many educational specialists have a direct impact on student learning whereas others have more of an indirect impact. For that reason, we offer two ways to approach the goal-setting process.

One approach to goal setting is to focus on student progress, whereas the other approach focuses on program progress. Although a school social worker does not teach students, she certainly will work to improve attendance, which is directly related to student achievement. A library/media specialist who makes sure that students have books at the appropriate reading level also impacts student learning, although this impact may be documented in a different way. In these two examples—a school social worker and a library/media specialist—the focus in goal setting is on the program rather than directly on the student. Please note that all educational programs should support student learning and, thus, are appropriate for the goal-setting process. We do recommend, however, that when an educational professional, whether it be a teacher or an educational specialist, can relate his or her work directly to student learning, then the focus of the goal should be student progress.

Figure 2.15 illustrates how an educational professional can create goals based on either student progress or on program progress. The language used in this example is provided merely as a guide to help bring clarity and specificity to the process so that the goal setting is transparent. The National Institute for Literacy, which endorses the use of goal setting, defines transparency as "an approach to teaching and learning in which the goals and purposes of learning, what will be learned, and what good performance looks like are clear and explicit to students, teachers, administrators, and other stakeholders."[20] Each step is documented with clear goals and clear indicators of what students should know and be able to do or in what ways the program should improve by the end of the year.[a]

---

a   Part II of this book provides numerous examples of both teacher and
     educational specialist goals.

Figure 2.15. Student Achievement/Program Progress Goal-Setting Template

		Student Progress	Program Progress
I.	Setting: Describe the population/program and special learning circumstances.	Add individualized statement about any relevant characteristics of the teacher's students, such as the percentages identified as special education, English language learners, performing below grade level, and performing above grade level.	Add individualized statement about any relevant characteristics of the educational specialist's work situation (i.e., school setting).
II.	Content Area: Describe the area/topic to be addressed.	Identify subject area objectives based on student achievement data.	Identify program area and objectives based on program assessment data.
III.	Baseline Data: Describe where the students are/program is at the beginning of the year.	Based on _____ (assessment measure of knowledge or skills) for _____ (school year), my students met/exceeded _____ (benchmark) in _____ (content area) but did not meet _____ (benchmark) in _____ (content area).	Based on _____ (measure of program progress) for _____ (school year), the program met/exceeded _____ in _____ (area) but did not meet _____ (benchmark) in _____ (area).
IV:	Goal Statement: Describe what should be accomplished by the end of the year.	In _____ (school year), _____ (a majority, or quantify with a percentage) of my students will meet _____ (benchmark) in _____ (content area). Additionally, all students will make acceptable measurable progress.	In _____ (school year), _____ (a majority or percentage) of my program will meet _____ (benchmark) in _____ (program area).

		Student Progress	Program Progress
V.	Strategies: Describe the activities that will be used to accomplish the goal.	I will use the following strategies to address student needs: (List strategies to be used.)	I will use the following strategies to address program needs: (List strategies to be used)
VI.	Mid-Year Review: Describe progress toward the goal at mid-year and any adjustments to strategies to be made.	At mid-year, my students have made/not made progress in _____ (content area) based on _____ (assessment measure of knowledge and skills). My students continue to need assistance in _____ (report on what still needs to be addressed). To make additional progress toward the goal, I will _____ (describe changes in strategies/additional strategies to be used).	At mid-year, the program has made/not made progress in _____ (area) based on _____ (measure of program progress). My program still experiences deficits in _____ (report on what still needs to be addressed). To make additional progress toward the goal, I will _____ (describe changes in strategies/additional strategies to be used).
VII.	End-of-Year Data Results: Describe goal attainment.	Based on _____ (assessment measure of knowledge or skills) for _____ (school year), my students met/exceeded _____ (benchmark) in _____ (content area) but did not meet _____ (benchmark) in _____ (content area).	Based on _____ (measure of program progress) for _____ (school year), the program met/exceeded _____ (benchmark) in _____ (area) but did not meet _____ (benchmark) in _____ (area).

How Can a Decision Tree Help in the Student Achievement Goal-Setting Process?

Student achievement goal setting is a process that provides a systematic way to focus on student learning and work toward improving student achievement of important curricular and learning outcomes. One way to develop goals and carry out the process systematically is by using a decision tree that shows the steps in the goal-setting process.

The student achievement goal-setting process in Figure 2.16 illustrates the steps discussed at the beginning of this chapter and also offers additional considerations for setting goals. Specifically, notice that in collecting data the teacher examines state assessment data, if available, but also relies on assessments that are closer to the classroom. This connection was shown when Teacher B used the state writing assessment results to examine whether a trend existed and then used a classroom-administered assessment to determine specific strengths and weaknesses. The shaded boxes are the defined steps discussed in this chapter, and the unshaded boxes provide additional incremental steps to consider.

Figure 2.16. Student Achievement Goal-Setting Decision Tree

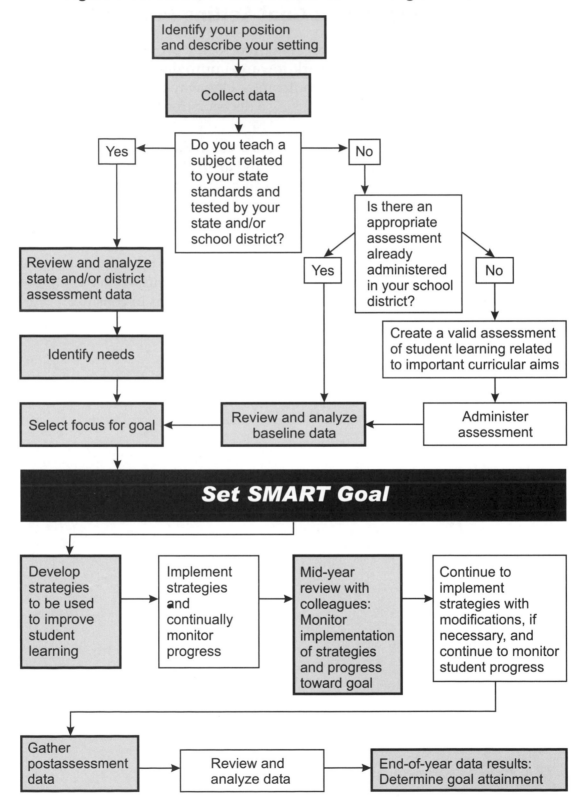

Summary

This chapter focused on how to implement student achievement goal setting. The five steps offered provide a systematic way to address the process and to provide purpose and direction. Documentation with a standardized format formalizes the process and makes goal setting transparent for the teacher or other educational professional. It can also make goal setting transparent for students, who can then be included in setting goals to achieve the knowledge and skills needed for success.

1   Education Week. (2008). *Standards, assessment, and accountability. Quality Counts 2008*. Retrieved May 1, 2008, from http://www.edweek.org/media/ew/qc/2008/18sos.h27.saa.pdf.

2   For a list of content standards from Virginia and Florida visit the following websites retrieved on May 1, 2008: Virginia Department of Education —http://www.doe.virginia.gov/VDOE/Superintendent/Sols/home.shtml; Florida Department of Education — http://www.fldoe.org/bii/curriculum/sss/

3   Education Week. (2008).

4   Gwinnett County Public Schools. (n.d.). *Academic knowledge and skills assessment program*. Retrieved May 20, 2008, from http://gwinnett.k12.ga.us/gcps-instruction 01.nsf/ImagesNavigators/F8080CC5B1B91339852571C70065213E/$file/2006-07Grade8promotion.pdf.

5   Maryland Department of Education. (n.d.). *High school assessment.* Retrieved May 20, 2008, from http://www.marylandpublicschools.org/MSDE/testing/hsa/.

6   Gall, M. D., Gall, J. P., & Borg, W. R. (2003). *Educational research: An introduction* (7th ed.), p. 389.

7   Barton, P. E. (2003). *Parsing the achievement gap: Baselines for tracking progress.* Princeton, NJ: Educational Testing Service.

8   Barton, P. E. (2003).

9   Dunkin, M. J. (1978). Student characteristics, classroom processes, and student achievement. *Journal of Educational Psychology, 70*(6), 998-1009.
    Dunkin, M. J. & Doenau, S. J. (1980). A replication study of unique and joint contributions to variance in student achievement. *Journal of Educational Psychology, 72*(3), 394 – 403.

10 Wright, S. P., Horn, S. P., & Sanders, W. L. (1997). Teacher and classroom context effects on student achievement: Implications for teacher evaluation. *Journals of Personnel Evaluation in Education, 11*(1), 57–67.

11 See, for example, Tomlinson, C. A. (1999). *The differentiated classroom: Responding to the needs of all learners.* Alexandria, VA: Association for Supervision and Curriculum Development.

12 Gillespie, M. K. (2002). *EFF research principle: A purposeful and transparent approach to teaching and learning* (EFF Research to Practice Note No. 1). Washington, DC: National Institute for Literacy.

13 Locke, E., & Latham, G. (1990). *A theory of goal setting and task performance.* Englewood Cliffs, NJ: Prentice-Hall.

14 See, for example, Good, T. L., & Brophy, J. E. (1997). *Looking in classrooms* (7th ed.). New York: Longman.
    Marzano, R. J., Pickering, D. J., & Pollock, J. E. (2001). *Classroom instruction that*

works: Research-based strategies for increasing student achievement. Alexandria, VA: Association for Supervision and Curriculum Development.

15 Marzano, R. J., Pickering, D. J., & Pollock, J. E. (2001).

16 Heffernan, L. (2004). *Critical literacy and writer's workshop.* Newark, DE: International Reading Association.

17 Stronge, J. H. (2007). *Qualities of effective teachers* (2nd ed.). Alexandria, VA: Association for Supervision and Curriculum Development.

18 Stiggins, R. J. (2002). Assessment crisis: The absence of assessment for learning. *Phi Delta Kappan 83*(10). Retrieved August 1, 2008 from http://electronicport folios.org/afl/Stiggins-AssessmentCrisis.pdf.

19 Little, J., Gearhart, M., Curry, M., & Kafka, J. (2003). Looking at student work for teacher learning, teacher community, and school reform. *Phi Delta Kappan, 85*(3), 185–192.

20 Gillespie, M. K. (2002). p. 8.

3

Using Data in Student Achievement Goal Setting

Introduction

The use of data provides the foundation for student achievement goal setting. Without the practical, timely, useful information provided by good data, a teacher or educational specialist would be like an archer shooting blindly at a target. The archer has to see the target to hit it. Likewise, a teacher or other educator has to know where students should be at the end of the year and chart their growth to get there. This chapter is not meant to serve as a guide for analyzing data because there are already many useful books on that topic. Rather, the purpose of the chapter is to examine possible data sources for student achievement goal setting and to provide guidelines for choosing those data sources. Specifically, this chapter addresses the following:

- ◆ Using data to assess student and/or program performance
- ◆ Assessment measures for student achievement goal setting
- ◆ Assessment measures for educators other than teachers

Using Data to Assess
Student and/or Program Performance

The most crucial argument for using data to assess student performance is that it results in improved student learning. In Chapter 1 we argued for the use of data to increase student performance, and we cited research studies to support this.

Data Defined

Throughout this chapter, we refer to the use of data in the student achievement goal-setting process. When we use the term "data," we mean *information gleaned from assessment measures that provides an indication of student progress and/or achievement.* Data can be collected in many forms, both quantitative and qualitative. Here are a few examples:

- Percentages
- Percentile rankings
- Grade equivalency scores
- Letter grades
- Performance level scores
- Written feedback on assignments
- Running records

Data are basically points of information used to make inferences about student learning. In student achievement goal setting these inferences are used to determine whether students have made progress over time.

The use of data to improve student performance is at the heart of teaching and learning. Assessment is not something done *only* at the end of instruction, it is inherent *to* instruction. In fact, teaching and assessing (i.e., instruction and analysis of learning) are so intertwined in effective teachers' classrooms that they are inseparable and almost indistinguishable at times.[1]

A review of research on effective teaching found that teachers who positively impact student learning tend to have the following traits:

♦ They are adept at using and creating a variety of assessments to monitor student learning.

♦ They frequently assess students.

♦ They understand how to interpret and use standardized assessment data and data from teacher-made assessments.

♦ They use assessment data to adjust instruction.[2]

These attributes are critical to student achievement goal setting. For teachers to set appropriate goals, they must have knowledge and skills in creating and using appropriate assessments and in analyzing and interpreting data.[3]

Challenges to using data must be addressed for student achievement goal setting to be successful. These challenges are described in Figure 3.1 below.

**Figure 3.1. Challenges to Proper Use
of Student Performance Data**

- Lack of teacher training in using assessment data either in preservice preparation or in professional development

- A culture that makes decisions based on anecdotal evidence or a "hunch" rather than on analysis of how well an instructional strategy is working

- A suspicion of the "gotcha" syndrome in which the use of data is merely to point out the "good" teachers and the "bad" teachers

- Lack of timely data available to teachers

- Lack of technology to make data easily accessible to teachers[4]

Assessment Measures
for Student Achievement Goal Setting

In this section of the chapter, we examine assessment measures that can be used for student achievement goal setting. Specifically we discuss the following:

- Guidelines for selecting assessment measures

- Methods of assessment

- Interpretation of assessment data

- Origination of assessments

- Organizing and displaying data for interpretation

Guidelines for Selecting Assessment Measures

Assessments are not all created equal. That is not an indictment against any one type of assessment; each serves its own purpose. In setting goals for student achievement or program improvement, we recommend the guidelines described in Figure 3.2.

Figure 3.2. Guidelines for the Use
of Student Performance Data in Goal Setting

♦ *The assessment must offer ways to preassess and postassess students' knowledge and skills.* The heart of student achievement goal setting is monitoring student learning and assessing the gains that students have made at the end of some period of time. Therefore, student growth must be documented through a pretest and a posttest of student learning.

♦ *The assessment must be cumulative in nature.* This guideline directly relates to the previous guideline, but it is important to make a special note here. Any assessment used for goal setting should measure the accumulation of knowledge and skills to measure growth.

♦ *The assessment and the data results from the assessment must be linked back to important curricular outcomes.* The assessment must be connected back to what the teacher intends for the students to learn. Most often, these curricular aims are defined by states and further defined by local school districts. Teachers, in turn, develop instructional objectives. The assessment must be aligned with the curricular aims at each level, and the data should link back to these curricular aims. In other words, the assessment must have curricular validity.[5]

♦ *Postassessment data must be available by the end of the time period for goal setting.* To determine goal attainment within the time period specified in the goal, the teacher or educational specialist must have access to postassessment data. Too often state or district-level high stakes test results are not available on a timely basis (i.e., by the end of the school year). Therefore, although the teacher and the entire school may work toward and be held accountable for performance on these end-of-course tests, the use of these tests as the sole measure for student achievement goal setting simply is not practical nor desirable.

Methods of Assessment

Obviously, there are different types of assessments and different ways to interpret assessment data. The two most common types of assessments include *criterion-referenced tests* and *norm-referenced tests.* Another type of assessment data includes *performance assessment* results. Performance assessment is essentially a criterion-referenced measure in that the performance is compared to a standard, just as student achievement of knowledge and skills is compared to instructional standards and goals. We separate the performance assessment from criterion-referenced measures because the latter are mostly thought of as paper-pencil types of measures, rather than authentic assessments of learning. Figure 3.3 describes the various types of assessment and provides examples of assessments that are often administered in pre-K–12 schools.

Figure 3.3. Methods and Attributes of Selected Student Assessment Measures

Method	Description	Scoring	Question Answered
Norm-referenced measures	Compare performance of student with performances of other students, classrooms, schools, school districts, and states	Scoring is based on the assumption that the skills or knowledge being measured are distributed in a way that resembles a normal bell curve	How are the students doing in comparison to others?
Criterion-referenced measures	Compare performance of student against instructional goals or standards	Scoring is based on the extent to which students demonstrate knowledge and skills at a predetermined level of performance	What do students know and what are they able to do?
Authentic assessment measures	Compare performance of student against performance standards under authentic conditions	Scoring can be based on (1) holistic judgments by teacher or expert panel, or (2) rubrics that delineate specific performance standards for each rating on a scale	How do students perform in school on a regular basis? How have students improved over time in an area of study? To what degree have students mastered the skill?

Figures 3.4 through 3.6 provide lists of potential student assessments for elementary, middle, and high school students.

**Figure 3.4. Sample Assessment Measures
for Elementary Teachers**

Subject Areas	Examples of Possible Student Achievement Measures
K–5 Reading	Dynamic Indicator of Basic Early Literacy Skills (DIBELS) Phonological Awareness Literacy Screening (PALS) School Readiness Uniform Screening System (SRUSS) STAR assessment data Scholastic Reading Inventory (SRI)
K–5 Mathematics	STAR assessment data
Science	Teacher-developed common assessments Performance assessments
Social Studies	Teacher-developed common assessments Performance assessments
Special Education	Measures for mathematics or reading (e.g., STAR, SRI, DIBELS) Individualized education plan (IEP) goal areas
Resource Areas: Music, Physical Education, Art	Performance assessments

Figure 3.5. Sample Assessment Measures for Middle Level Teachers

Subject Areas	Examples of Possible Student Achievement Measures
Language Arts	Reading measures (e.g., STAR, SRI) Benchmark district-wide assessments Teacher-developed assessments (e.g., achievement tests, performance assessments, skills checklists)
Mathematics	STAR assessment data Benchmark district-wide assessments Teacher-developed assessments (e.g., achievement tests, performance assessments, skills checklists)
Social Studies	Benchmark district-wide assessments Teacher-developed assessments
Science	Benchmark district-wide assessments Teacher-developed assessments
Special Education	Reading or mathematics measures (e.g., STAR, SRI) IEP goal areas Appropriate standardized measurements
Resource Areas: Physical Education, Art, Music, Technical Education	Student performance in district and regional competitions (adjudicated) Presidential fitness tests Performance assessments with valid rubrics
Foreign Language	Benchmark district-wide assessments Teacher-developed assessments

Figure 3.6. Sample Assessment Measures for High School Teachers

Subject Areas	Examples of Possible Student Achievement Measures
English	Benchmark district-wide assessments Teacher-developed assessments (e.g., achievement tests, performance assessments, skills checklists) International Baccalaureate (IB) exams (previously administered or practice tests) Advanced Placement (AP) exams (previously administered or practice tests)
Mathematics	Benchmark district-wide assessments Teacher-developed assessments (e.g., achievement tests, performance assessments, skills checklists) IB exams (previously administered or practice tests) AP exams (previously administered or practice tests)
Social Studies	Benchmark district-wide assessments Teacher-developed assessments IB exams AP exams
Science	Benchmark district-wide assessments Teacher-developed assessments IB exams AP exams
Special Education	Reading or mathematics measures (e.g., STAR, SRI) IEP goal areas Appropriate standardized measurements
Art, Music, Physical Education, Technical Education, Career Education	Student performance in regional and district competitions (adjudicated) Presidential fitness tests Industry exams (i.e., driver's education) Benchmark district-wide assessments Teacher-developed assessments
Foreign Language	Benchmark district-wide assessments Teacher-developed assessments IB exams AP exams

Interpretation of Assessment Data

Data gleaned from each type of assessment must be interpreted in different ways, and this interpretation informs the goal-setting process. For example, answering 50 percent of questions correctly on a test has far different implications than scoring in the 50th percentile. Additionally, scoring at a "basic" level of performance on sight-singing in music warrants interpretation. What does "basic" mean? Is "basic" acceptable? Figure 3.7 provides information to assist in interpreting assessment data and setting goals.

Figure 3.7. Types of Assessment and their Application to Goal Setting

Types of Assessment	Appropriate Interpretation for a Single Student	Appropriate Goal
Norm-referenced measures	Jerome is at the 68th percentile on the Stanford 10 Reading Test. This means that Jerome scored better than 68% of the norm group (or, conversely, 32% of the norm group scored better than him). This score does not indicate the knowledge and skills that Jerome does or does not have in reading.	In the current school year, students in the lowest quartile (less than 25th percentile) on the state reading norm-referenced test will improve by 10 percentile points on the state reading norm-referenced test.
Criterion-referenced measures	Jerome answered 20 of the 25 questions on reading comprehension correctly. This means that Jerome answered 80% of the questions correctly. This score does not indicate the relative ranking of Jerome to his classmates.	In the current school year, 80% of my students will meet the benchmarks established in the five strand areas on the mathematics district-wide proficiency test. Additionally, all of my students' scores will improve.

Types of Assessment	Appropriate Interpretation for a Single Student	Appropriate Goal
Authentic assessment measures	Jerome scored at a basic level on a four-level holistic rubric in his ability to write an essay. This means that Jerome's performance is based on a set criterion associated with performance levels. Authentic assessment data results are interpreted similarly to criterion-referenced assessments.	In the current school year, 80% of my students will score at a proficient level in essay writing according to the state writing rubric for scoring. All of my students will demonstrate measurable growth in writing by improving by at least one level.

Origination of Assessments

Multiple assessment measures exist in most grades and in many subject areas. Students are being tested more than ever in our current educational climate. However, as any effective teacher, principal, or other educator knows, testing is not a key to learning: administering and using the correct tests is. The key to the effective use of student achievement goal setting is choosing the most appropriate assessment measure given the circumstances of both the curriculum and the students. The types of assessment measures that are often available to teachers on a day-to-day basis include the following:

- Standardized assessment measures
- District-wide assessment measures
- Teacher-developed assessment measures

Each type of assessment can be a paper-pencil exam with multiple-choice items, short answers, or extended-response items. Alternatively, each type could be a more authentic measure of student learning, and these might include writing an essay, conducting an experiment, analyzing a primary source document, and so forth.

Standardized Assessments

Standardized assessments can be either criterion-referenced or norm-referenced. Criterion-referenced assessments include state-customized assessments such as the Washington Assessment of Student Learning (WASL) and the California Achievement Test (CAT). Norm-referenced assessments include tests such as the Iowa Test of Basic Skills (ITBS) and the Stanford 10. These assessments serve different purposes, but both are standardized, meaning they have been tested for validity and reliability and are designed, administered, scored, and interpreted according to preestablished protocols. The following list provides pros and cons of using standardized test data for student achievement goal setting.

- ♦ *Pros:* Standardized assessments are, of course, standardized. They have been tested for validity and reliability. State-customized assessments have high degrees of content validity because they are developed to measure student learning according to state standards. Some standardized assessments such as PALS or DIBELS provide for progress monitoring of student growth.

- ♦ *Cons:* Standardized assessments measure a very broad swath of curricular outcomes and are not as useful in diagnosing specific strengths and weaknesses of students. State-customized assessments typically assess a discrete set of knowledge and skills and thus it is difficult to determine growth from one year to the next unless scores are vertically equated (see sidebar). Also, the data may not be received for individual students or it may not arrive in a timely fashion, preventing the teacher from determining goal attainment.

In considering both the pros and cons, we recommend that standardized assessment data be used to help provide a focal area for the goal rather than to provide baseline data for individual students. Standardized assessments typically do not allow for pre- and posttesting of students. To make the case, consider the standardized assessment data in Figure 3.8 in which the national percentile ranking is provided for a student who took the Stanford 10 test.

Vertical Equating of Grade-Level Tests

As of 2008, 24 states vertically equate scores on math and reading state-customized assessments for Grades 3 through 8.[6]

A vertically equated score is a score that can provide an indication of student growth over time. States may do this in two ways.

1. The state of Florida uses a developmental scale score to determine student growth. By knowing the increase in developmental scale score points from one year to the next, the teacher has an idea of whether the student grew at least one year in reading or mathematics.[7]

2. The state of Pennsylvania uses a value-added assessment system in which factors related to student achievement, such as prior achievement, are factored into a model and a prediction is made as to what the student's score *should be* based on the factors. The predicted score is then compared to the actual score.[8]

Although these two methods for vertically equating scores provide evidence of growth, they are still unable to pinpoint specific strengths and weaknesses.

**Figure 3.8. Sample Student Score
on Stanford 10 Test**

Sub-Area	National Percentile Ranking
Reading	88
Math	95
Language	54
Partial Battery	77

Based on the data in Figure 3.8, this student performs well overall and is above average in all subject areas compared to the norm group. She clearly is strong in mathematics as shown by scoring in the 95th percentile. Her language abilities in the areas of grammar, punctuation, and writing are weaker, and she scores at the 54th percentile on this portion of the test. Therefore, we can draw the conclusion that this child would benefit from focused language work as well as continued work in reading and mathematics. What this information does not tell us, however, is what areas of language specifically challenge the student. In goal setting, a teacher should set baseline data by administering an assessment that provides specific information about the strengths and weaknesses in language subareas.

District-Developed Assessment Measures

Many districts administer district-wide assessments to gauge the degree to which students and entire classes are achieving according to state standards. These assessments are often referred to as "benchmark assessments," "short-cycle assessments," or "interim assessments." These assessments are not necessarily standardized and are usually developed by a team at the district level.[9]

- ♦ *Pros:* Typically, district-wide assessments are tied directly to curricular aims, and the data can be provided to teachers in a timely fashion. These types of assessments are typically given each nine weeks or for some other determined period of time to document student achievement of knowledge and skills.

- ♦ *Cons:* District-wide assessments may have lower degrees of validity and reliability than standardized assessments, depending on their development. Additionally, district-developed assessments must be cumulative in nature to provide evidence of student growth over time. Some districts may develop assessments that measure a discrete set of knowledge and skills for the marking period rather than track growth over time.

Figure 3.9 provides an example of how a district might report student's performance on a third-grade mathematics benchmark assessment.

**Figure 3.9. Sample Student Results
from District Benchmark Assessment**

State Mathematics Curriculum Strand	Score (Percent Correct)
Number and Number Sense	69
Computation and Estimation	67
Measurement	100
Probability and Statistics	40
Patterns, Functions, and Algebra	63

The data show that the student needs assistance in virtually each strand except measurement. Specifically, probability and statistics are of major concern and would be an area targeted for intervention. The teacher is able to link the score back to the state curriculum strands and to the state curriculum standards. However, unless this test is cumulative in nature it does not show growth over time.

Teacher-Developed Assessment Measures

Teacher-developed measures include tests, quizzes, performance assessments, projects, or any other assessment to be used for formative and/or summative purposes. Teachers conduct informal assessments, such as observations of students identifying plant parts under the correct category, as well as formal assessments, such as a history test on the Civil War. Teachers use data from small-group discussion, whole-group discussion, homework assignments, and interest surveys to prepare students for learning and to make instructional decisions.[10] These are informal types of data. Assessments for student achievement goal setting should be more formal in nature, but they should also be formative so that the data can be used to diagnose and address students' weaknesses.

Teachers can develop assessments individually or in teams. For example, third-grade teachers could develop common assessments to track student progress in mathematics or reading. The social studies department in a high school could develop common assessments to track student progress in historical analysis skills.

- ♦ *Pros:* Teacher-developed assessments are closer to the student and thus closer to the learning that is taking place in the classroom. They can be responsive to the various learning styles and needs of the learners and can be adjusted for pacing of instruction. Teacher-developed assessments can also be tied more closely to the intended curricular aims that were actually taught, giving a clear picture of what students have learned as a result of instruction. Additionally, teachers can create and administer more authentic assessments of student learning, such as the ability to carry out a scientific experiment.

♦ *Cons:* The validity and reliability of teacher-developed assessments depend on the assessment skills of individual teachers. Additionally, it is virtually impossible to compare student performance across teachers or classes unless the tests are jointly designed and administered in a standard format.

If the assessments are developed in a way that will provide useful data, teacher-developed assessments can be a powerful tool in student achievement goal setting.[a] Therefore, despite their inherent limitations, we recommend including their use in student achievement goal setting.

Figure 3.10 shows results from an assessment of a student's abilities in scientific investigation. The teacher developed a four-level rubric and used it to score an experiment.

Figure 3.10. Sample Student Results from Scientific Investigation Performance Assessment

Criteria	Score*	Teacher Comments
Hypothesis	3	*The hypothesis was sufficiently developed and provided direction to the investigation.*
Investigation Design	3	*The investigation was well constructed and could be replicated by another individual.*
Methods of Data Collection	3	*Adequate and accurate data was collected, recorded, and displayed in an organized fashion.*
Data Analysis	2	*The results provided some relationship to the hypothesis; inferences and recommendations were inconsistent with the findings.*

*1 = below basic; 2 = basic; 3 = developing; 4 = mastery.

The teacher using the data in Figure 3.10 has a great deal of information to draw from in making inferences about student learning. The student has the ability to

---

a   For a detailed explanation of how teachers can create valid and reliable assessments see: Gareis, C. R., & Grant, L. W. (2008). *Teacher-made assessments: How to connect curriculum, instruction, and student learning.* Larchmont, NY: Eye On Education.

design and carry out an experiment but falls short on analyzing the data, making appropriate inferences, and drawing supported conclusions. Therefore, the teacher knows that the student needs assistance in this area. Furthermore, these same types of data can be collected at a later time to determine whether the student has grown in the area of data analysis. In fact, using a skills checklist can be an excellent tool to monitor individual student or whole-group progress over time. An example of such a skills checklist is provided in Figure 3.11.

Figure 3.11. Sample Sub-Skills Checklist

Skill Area: Generating Hypotheses			
Class: 3rd period			
Student	**Date/Score***	**Date/Score**	**Date/Score**	**Date/Score**
Student A	Sep 6/**2**	Sep 12/**3**	Sep 22/**3**	Oct 4/**3**
Student B	Sep 6/**3**	Sep 12/**3**	Sep 22/**4****	—
Student C	Sep 7/**2**	Sep 12/**3**	Sep 22/**3**	Oct 4/**4**
Student D	Sep 6/**1**	Sep 12/**2**	Sep 22/**3**	Oct 4/**3**
Student E	Sep 7/**3**	Sep 12/**4****	—	—

*1 = below basic; 2 = basic; 3 = developing; 4 = mastery.

**Note: No additional skill assessment was required after mastery was achieved.

A review of research that examined the use of curriculum-based measurement (CBM) data found that merely collecting data might not be enough to affect student achievement.[11] Grouping student performance data by subskills can create a more powerful effect on student achievement. Teachers can then target specific areas for improvement. In Figure 3.11, the teacher has a clear indication of whether students are experiencing success or difficulty with the subskill as well as a running record of their performance over time.

Standardized assessments can be created at the national or state level, and other assessments can be created at the district level or by individual teachers. Figure 3.12 provides a summary overview of the pros and cons of each type.

**Figure 3.12. Pros and Cons of Each Type of Assessment
for Student Achievement Goal Setting**

Type of Assessment	Pros	Cons
Standardized Assessments	• Tested for validity and reliability • Standardized approach to testing • Ability to compare student performance across teachers and classes	• Tests broad swath of curricular outcomes • Difficult to diagnose specific strengths and weaknesses of students • Difficult to track growth over time • Data received long after test given
District-wide Assessments	• Results may be directly tied to curricular aims • Ability to compare student performance across teachers and classes • Data can be provided in a timely fashion • Administered throughout the year	• May have lower degrees of validity and reliability than standardized assessments • May not be cumulative in nature and therefore may not provide evidence of student growth over time
Teacher-Developed Assessments	• Based on curricular aims actually taught in the classroom • Can be used to guide and pace instruction • May be more authentic measures of student learning	• May have lower degrees of validity and reliability, depending on the assessment skills of the teacher • Difficult to compare student performance across teachers or classes

Organizing and Displaying Data for Interpretation

There are many ways to organize and display data. Regardless of the method selected, a visual display of data is a powerful tool for interpretation. Specific data presentation methods to organize and display findings might include data tables (e.g., raw data and compiled data) and graphical depictions of data, each of which will be illustrated below.

Raw Data

Raw data might include a table of all students by class and their scores and subscores on assessments. Figure 3.13 offers an example of raw data in which the teacher provides the grade equivalency scores for each student according to the STAR reading assessment. This assessment is given as pre- and post-forms to track students' improvement in reading. The raw data provide a clear indication of which students have improved greatly and which students have made more modest progress.

Figure 3.13. Example of Raw Data Display
Using STAR Reading Assessment Data

Student	August Pre-Test GE*	December Mid-Year GE	May End-of-Year GE	Pre-Post Change in GE (from August to May)
Brian	1.2	1.4	1.9	0.7
Calvin	0.9	1.2	1.5	0.6
Jake	2.4	2.6	2.9	0.5
José	1.8	2.4	3.1	1.3
Ilner	1.9	2.6	3.3	1.4
Mike	0.7	0.9	1.2	0.5
Stephon	2.1	2.5	2.9	0.8
Tasha	2.3	2.5	3.2	0.9
Veronica	2.5	2.7	3.6	1.1
Average	**1.74**	**2.08**	**2.62**	**0.88**

*GE = Grade equivalency

Compiled Data Tables

Compiled data tables provide information in table form similar to raw data, but they also combine groups of students in some way. For example, compiled data tables might include information such as the following:

♦ Percent of students at a given benchmark, that is, grade level or proficiency level

♦ Average percentile scores for students on subareas or content strands of an assessment

♦ Average scaled scores for subscales and total battery

♦ Percent of students within quartiles on a norm-referenced assessment

Figure 3.14 provides an example of a compiled data table. Students' persuasive and expository writing were scored using a six-level rubric. Although each student's score is not listed, the compiled data provide an indication of the performances of various students within a category. This is a helpful way for the teacher to display the data because it gives him or her an idea of whether the overall class has shown improvement from the beginning of the year.

Figure 3.14. Number and Percent of Students Earning Each Score Point on Essay Prompts*

	Number and Percent of Students Earning Each Score Point on the Essays						
	Unscorable	1	2	3	4	5	6
Expository: Baseline	3 (5%)	7 (12%)	12 (21%)	19 (33%)	8 (14%)	5 (9%)	3 (5%)
Expository: End of Year*	0 (0%)	2 (4%)	5 (9%)	11 (19%)	29 (51%)	6 (11%)	4 (7%)
Persuasive: Baseline	2 (3%)	9 (16%)	14 (25%)	21 (37%)	5 (9%)	4 (7%)	2 (3%)
Persuasive: End of Year*	0 (0%)	1 (2%)	8 (14%)	18 (32%)	16 (28%)	9 (16%)	5 (9%)

*Percentages do not equal 100 as a result of rounding.

Graphs of Compiled Data

Graphs of compiled data are a powerful visual tool to show how students are performing in a given area. Graphs can include line, bar, stacked bar, and pie graphs, to name a few of the more commonly used types. The type of data and the nature of the data can vary. Data can be for a given year, by quartiles or by successive grade level groups, and it can be disaggregated based on minority or gender status. Data can also be provided over time to include successive grade level groups or monitoring of the same group of students. Additionally, trend data can be disaggregated by minority or gender status, or by using the groups associated with adequate yearly progress (AYP) under No Child Left Behind (NCLB). Whatever the intent, a timely, well-designed, and appropriate graph can illuminate findings in a way that numbers alone cannot. The old adage that a picture paints a thousand words does seem to hold true.

Figure 3.15 provides an example of a graph of compiled data. This graph shows the baseline and end-of-year data for the expository writing scores from data in Figure 3.14. By quickly looking at the graph, one can tell that the class as a whole has made progress, with more students scoring a "3" or below in August and more students scoring a "4" or above in May.

**Figure 3.15. Number of Students Scoring
at Corresponding Performance Levels on a Writing Prompt**

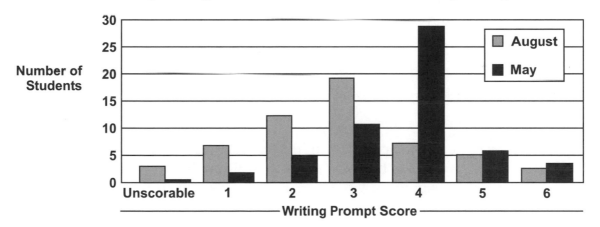

Assessment Measures for Goal Setting
for Educators Other Than Teachers

Up to this point, we have primarily emphasized classroom examples of student achievement. However, there are many instances in which school-based, nonteaching educators have an impact on student and school success, although not in a manner that can be directly connected to student achievement. For example, educational specialists such as instructional coaches, guidance counselors, library/media specialists, and others may work with a large group of students or a vital educational program. In these cases it can be appropriate to use both student achievement measures as well as measures related to overall program progress.

Student Achievement Measures

Despite its limitations, we do advocate the use of standardized achievement data in some cases. For example, an instructional coach who oversees the mathematics program in a school by providing professional development, modeling teaching strategies, and working with individual students may use standardized achievement data from the entire school if he or she is given the responsibility of increasing mathematics achievement. In this case, whole-school standardized achievement data may be appropriate to use.

Measures that Correlate with Student Achievement

Other measures that correlate with student achievement may also be used if the measures are associated with the educational specialists' work. For example, a school social worker's job might be to decrease truancy, thereby increasing attendance of chronically absent students. It would be appropriate to use attendance statistics as a measure for the social worker's goal. Other measures that correlate with student achievement include the following:

- ♦ Dropout rates
- ♦ Graduation rates
- ♦ Number and/or nature of discipline referrals
- ♦ Job-placement rates

This list of performance measures that are related to, but not direct measures of, student achievement can be modified depending on the particular educational area and the specific assignment. Goal setting can (and should) extend to all educational professionals in the school.

Program Measures

Many educational specialists administer programs that would be difficult to tie directly to student achievement. For example, although a library/media specialist at the high school level could theoretically be tied to student achievement in reading, it is difficult to measure the value-added effect of library/media specialists directly on student achievement. However, library/media specialists are assigned the important responsibility of making instructional tools and resources available to students and teachers to do their work. Thus, the library/media specialists are one step removed from student achievement. Consequently, a reasonable alternative to student achievement may need to be considered to give these educational specialists an opportunity to demonstrate their impact on school or student success. Thus, we turn to program progress rather than direct student progress. Examples of program measures include the following:

- Participant evaluations of professional development programs
- Use of resources such as percentage of time library is in use or number of books checked out per year
- Time period between identification for child study and determination of special education eligibility
- Percentage or number of students and/or staff using services

These measures offer a way for educational specialists to improve on the programs they administer that support student learning. Figure 3.16 provides examples of possible measures that may be appropriate for educational specialists.

Figure 3.16. Possible Measures for Goal Setting for Educational Specialists

Educational Specialist Position	Sample Assessment Measures
Library Media Specialists	• Standardized assessment data, if appropriate • Accelerated reader program data • Library use measures
Guidance Counselors	• Standardized assessment data, if appropriate • Student attendance • Discipline referral rates • Graduation rates
Instructional Coaches	• Standardized assessment data • Professional development session evaluations
School Psychologists	• Standardized assessment data, if appropriate • Individualized education plan (IEP) goal tracking • Report logs

Educational Specialist Position	Sample Assessment Measures
School Social Workers	• Attendance records • Discipline referrals • Dropout rates
Physical/ Occupational Therapists	• Industry assessments • IEP goal tracking • Therapy logs
Speech/Language Pathologists	• Industry assessments • IEP goal tracking

Summary

An understanding of assessment and its uses is central to choosing appropriate data sources. Although goals can be based on student progress data, other measures related to student progress and/or program progress data can need to be considered in some instances. The type of data used will depend on the position and goal orientation of the educational professional. Regardless of the type of goal established, assessment measures should do the following:

♦ Allow for pre- and postassessment of students' knowledge and skills

♦ Link back to important curricular aims

♦ Allow for goal determination within a specified time period

♦ Be cumulative in nature

1 Stronge, J. H. (2007). *Qualities of effective teachers.* (2nd ed.). Alexandria, VA: Association for Supervision and Curriculum Development.

2 Stronge, J. H. (2007).

3 Gareis, C. R., & Grant, L.W. (2008). *Teacher-made assessments: How to connect curriculum, instruction, and student learning.* Larchmont, NY: Eye On Education.

4 Lachat, M. A., & Smith, S. (2005). Practices that support data use in urban high schools. *Journal of Education for Students Placed At Risk, 10*(3), 333–349. Schmoker, M. (1996). *Results: The key to continuous school improvement.* Alexandria, VA: Association for Supervision and Curriculum Development.

5 Gareis, C. R., & Grant, L. W. (2008).

6 Education Week. (2008). Standards, Assessment, and Accountability. *Quality Counts 2008.* Retrieved May 1, 2008, from http://www.edweek.org/media/ew/qc/2008/18sos.h27.saa.pdf.

7 Florida Department of Education. (n.d.). Assessment and school performance. In *Frequently asked questions.* Retrieved May 20, 2008, from http://www.fldoe.org/faq/default.asp?Dept=179&ID=985#Q985.

8 Pennsylvania Department of Education. (n.d.). *Pennsylvania value-added assessment system.* Retrieved May 20, 2008, from http://www.pde.state.pa.us/a_and_t/cwp/view.asp?a–108&Q–108916&a_and_tNav=I6429I&a_and_tNav=I.

9 Bambrick-Santoyo, P. (2008). Data in the driver's seat. *Educational Leadership, 65*(4), 43–47.

10 Tomlinson, C. A. (1999). *The differentiated classroom: Responding to the needs of all learners.* Alexandria, VA: Association for Supervision and Curriculum Development.

11 Stecker, P. M., Fuchs, L. S., & Fuchs, D. (2005). Using curriculum-based measurement to improve student achievement: Review of research. *Psychology in the Schools, 42*(8), 795–819.

4

How to Implement Student Achievement Goal Setting

Introduction

In Chapter 1 we asserted that education is about improving the quality of life for students. How do we add value to our students' lives? The short answer is that we do so through teaching (in all its myriad forms) and through learning. The quandary we have, however, is this: What works in teaching and learning? As we know from extensive research across many decades[1] and from our own experiences, some instructional methods and strategies work very well, and some don't. Some methods work well with some students but not with others. Some work well in certain settings and in certain ways, but not in all settings and in all ways. So, what are we to do? Given the extraordinary complexity of teaching and learning, if we are indeed to change the lives of our students in positive and lasting ways, we must find what works best with our students.

In this concluding chapter to Part I of Student Achievement Goal Setting: Using Data to Improve Teaching and Learning, we address a number of issues related to the implementation of goal setting. In particular, we consider the following issues:

- ♦ What student achievement goal setting can't do

- ♦ Practical guidelines for using student achievement goal setting

- ♦ The importance of professional development in implementing student achievement goal setting

What Student Achievement Goal Setting Can't Do

Up to this point, we have focused on what student achievement goal setting is, how to use it, and its potential benefits to teaching and learning. However, our discussion would be incomplete if we did not touch on what goal setting cannot do.

Despite the many potential benefits of growth models such as student achievement goal setting in documenting and facilitating student learning, there are limitations. In particular, Popham offered a note of caution about the use of formative assessment, which is a key component in goal setting:

> Although formative assessment is a wonderful, research-rooted way for teachers to teach better and for learners to learn better, it is unlikely to make much of a difference when it comes to increasing students' scores on inappropriate accountability tests, especially those that are instructionally insensitive.[2]

In his book *Transformative Assessment*, Popham stated that "instructionally inappropriate accountability tests not only fail to supply an accurate evaluation of school quality but also may lead some teachers to engage in student-harmful instructional practices, such as excessive test preparation or the elimination of curricular content."[3] We contend that formative uses of student assessment, such as those applied in student achievement goal setting, are at the very heart of student learning, teacher quality performance, and school improvement. Although formative assessment—and by extension student achievement goal setting—may not directly impact high-stakes test results if those accountability tests are inappropriately designed or applied, we should not abandon this highly productive and promising form of student assessment.

Standardized tests do serve a purpose if they are valid and reliable measures of student achievement. However, as Popham states in his discussion of the Uncertainty Principle, the more something is measured the more distorted it becomes. Standardized tests can provide an overall picture of a student's performance (e.g., whether the student is stronger in math or reading, whether the student has greater knowledge of science or social studies content, etc.). What standardized tests do not provide is a picture of the specific strengths and weaknesses within each subject area.

Guidelines for Using Student Achievement Goal Setting

Whenever student growth is assessed, it is essential that acceptable methods for documenting learning growth are used (e.g., pre- and postassessment). Figure 4.1 summarizes six key considerations for incorporating student achievement or other measures of student performance in goal setting.

Figure 4.1. Guidelines for Using Student Achievement Goal Setting[4]

1. *Use fair and valid measures of student learning.*

   Reliability, validity, freedom from bias, and fairness are obvious concerns and conditions for assessing student performance. These criteria for test selection are essential conditions for a proper testing program.

2. *Use measures of student growth rather than a fixed achievement standard or goal.*

   A growth orientation requires the use of pre- and posttesting to determine progress rather than the attainment of predetermined pass rates or proficiency levels based on a single performance. True measures of learning should focus on growth in knowledge and skills, not on single aptitude scores.

3. *Compare learning gains from one point in time to another for the same students, not different groups of students.*

   Implicit in the concept of gain scores is the assumption that similar tests will be used to measure student learning across time on an individual basis. When multiple measures of student learning are aggregated across the same class of students, a fairer measure of student learning gains can be generated.

4. *Recognize that gain scores have pitfalls that must be avoided.*

   Even when measures of student growth are used, it is important to interpret gain scores properly. In particular, a statistical artifact known as the regression effect needs to be considered. It results in a tendency for students starting with low performance levels to show larger gains than warranted and students with higher performance to show lower gains. Both groups regress to the mean or average performance. Additionally, a ceiling effect on the test will interfere with students who start with high scores, as the ceiling makes it difficult to show continued high gain scores.

5. *Select student assessment measures that are most closely aligned with the existing curriculum.*

    Standardized tests should be selected based on their general or predominant alignment with the articulated curriculum. The more closely aligned the assessment measures are with the curriculum, the more accurate they are as a gauge of student learning.

6. *Do not narrow the curriculum and limit teaching to fit a test unless the test actually measures what should be taught.*

    This is another unintended but predictable consequence of selecting standardized tests that are not aligned with the curriculum is the distortion of the curriculum to meet the demands of the test. Curriculum and instruction should drive assessment, not the reverse.

The Importance of Professional Development in Implementing Student Achievement Goal Setting

In a study of a group of schools in the San Francisco area, the researchers found that the frequency with which teachers collected, interpreted, and analyzed data for instructional improvement distinguished schools that were closing the achievement gap from those that were not. Additionally, the researchers found that "two-thirds of the teachers surveyed in the gap-closing schools said they used tests and other data at least several times a month to understand their students' skills gaps, and sometimes several times a week."[5] It seems clear that "instructional responsiveness to student assessments is a powerful tool for increased student achievement."[6] However, this claim is predicated on the rather tenuous assumption that teachers are appropriately prepared to do the important work of collecting, interpreting, analyzing, and using student achievement data to drive instruction. This may or may not be true.

Why Teachers Need Support to Implement Goal Setting

Some teachers are already well equipped to use student achievement goal setting. (See Figure 4.2 for examples of teachers who typically use instructional processes that are comparable to student achievement goal setting.) However, for many teachers and administrators, goal setting will be a novelty. Undoubtedly, they will need help—especially in the form of ongoing professional development—if they are to successfully implement the goal-setting process.

Figure 4.2. Teacher Groups that Currently Use Goal-Setting Processes

Teacher Group	Ways in Which They Use Goal Setting (e.g., preassessment, instruction, postassessment)
First-Grade Teachers	• Preassessment on reading skills • Differentiated instruction based on skills • Reading skills checklist updated regularly • Ongoing skills assessments
Special Education Teachers	• Diagnostic assessment on academic skills • Development of individual education plan (IEP) based on assessment • Individualized instruction based on IEP • Ongoing monitoring of student progress • Modifications of IEP as needed
Athletic Coaches (e.g., football coaches)	• Assessment of player skills during preseason • Assignment of players to specific positions based on skills assessment • Ongoing assessment/instruction/assessment throughout playing season

What Types of Support Do Teachers Need to Implement Goal Setting?

As with any substantive change in teacher practice, student achievement goal setting will require substantial support for the many teachers for whom the goal-setting process is not part of their training or current practice. Solid support must be operationalized in practical terms and should include the following:

♦ Comprehensive professional development opportunities;

♦ Ongoing commitment and encouragement from administrators;

♦ Opportunities to experiment with what works; and

♦ The necessary resources to understand and then use the process (e.g., technical assistance, student data provided in useable forms, etc.).

It is very important to accompany implementation of goal setting with high-quality professional development. Because goal setting is both a standardized process (as discussed in Chapter 2) and customized to fit the unique learning needs of a given group of students, the professional development also should have these features. Standardized training for all teachers as well as embedded (i.e., customized) teacher learning opportunities should be included.

When it comes to using student achievement data, teachers often examine student work on their own and in isolation from colleagues. Fortunately, in recent years educational reformers and professional developers have begun bringing teachers together to look at student work collaboratively.[7] In a series of case studies, researchers examined teacher groups in four school sites to identify specific practices used in collaborative teacher efforts to look at student work. Their findings yielded three common elements in these collaborative teacher groups:

1. The schools brought teachers together to focus on student learning and teaching practice. Specifically, teachers reserved time and space in their regular work schedule to talk about student learning and teaching practices that took place in the course of their ongoing school work.

2. The teachers focused on getting student work on the table and into the conversation rather than merely in teachers' instructional materials, lesson plans, and so forth.

3. The teachers structured the conversations around student learning, and their teaching practice used protocols (procedural steps and guidelines) to help organize the discussion.[8]

All three of these steps would likely prove helpful in organizing teacher professional development efforts for student achievement goal setting.

Professional development can be a key to the successful implementation of any program. For professional development to be successful it must have the following characteristics:

♦ Timeliness—It should be related to the current work of the teacher.

♦ Relevance—It should be related to the teacher's area of focus.

♦ Interaction—It should provide time for practice and hands-on learning.[9]

When using student achievement goal setting, teachers must receive training about the steps involved in the process and about using their own student achievement data in the subject areas they teach.

Helping Students Apply Goal-Setting Techniques

Naturally, when we consider training for implementing a reform or a new strategy, we typically think of teachers and administrators as the frontline for implementation. However, if we want the most return for our investment in the reform effort, we need to consider providing training for the students themselves.

In implementing a standards-based approach to teacher evaluation, a school district in Thompson, Colorado, found that students who learned growth and performance standards began understanding—and applying—standards to their own learning: "Students in their own language are talking about standards. They know what is expected of them and what they should be able to do."[10] Commenting on student ownership of achievement, Good and Brophy noted that "goal setting must be accompanied by goal commitment. Students must take the goals seriously and commit themselves to trying to reach them."[11]

When students understand what they need to know and then take ownership for their learning, we have made a major step toward student success. Thus, it is incumbent that educators teach students the value of a goals-based learning environment. The way that teachers provide performance feedback to students can impact the students' ability to understand and respond to learning goals. Consider, for example, the simple matter of how grades are communicated:

> When giving students feedback on both oral and written work, it is the nature, rather than the amount, of commentary that is critical. Research experiments have established that, although student learning can be advanced by feedback through comments, the giving of numerical scores or grades has a negative effect, in that students ignore comments when marks are also given.[12] These results often surprise teachers, but those who have abandoned the giving of marks discover that their experience confirms the findings: Students do engage more productively in improving their work.[13]

Whether teachers make only slight changes to their practice (such as how they give feedback to students) or more substantively and directly teach students to understand and own their own learning goals, students must be part of the goal setting equation if the maximum benefits are to be realized.

Conclusion

Given the importance of improving performance for all students, the fundamental question that we must ask about accountability efforts in general and instructional strategies in particular is, does it work? As we bring this part of the book to a close, we want to revisit the broader issue of accountability in schools. Again, we would contend that, within certain constraints, a balanced focus on improvement and accountability for both students and teachers does yield academic growth. To illustrate the relationship between accountability efforts and student achievement, consider the following state-by-state analysis:

> We developed a zero-to-five index of the strength of accountability in 50 states based on the use of high-stakes testing to sanction and reward schools, and analyzed whether that index is related to student gains on the NAEP mathematics test in 1996–2000....The results show that students in high-accountability states averaged significantly greater gains

on the NAEP eighth-grade math test than students in states with little or no state measures to improve student performance.[14]

Given the central role that teachers have always played in successful schools, connecting teacher work and student performance is a logical extension of the educational reform agenda.[15] "The purpose of teaching is learning, and the purpose of schooling is to ensure that each new generation of students accumulates the knowledge and skills needed to meet the social, political, and economic demands of adulthood."[16] It is this teaching and learning connection that is the ultimate focus of student achievement goal setting.

We haven't attempted to portray student achievement goal setting as the solution for all our learning needs. Indeed, no program, strategy, or approach in education can legitimately support such a claim. However, we do offer student achievement goal setting as one well-tested method that has proven effective in various forms and various settings. More importantly, we hope it will help improve both teaching and learning for students in your school.

1 See, for example, Good, T. L., & Brophy, J. E. (1997). *Looking in classrooms* (7th ed.). New York: Longman.
Marzano, R. J., Pickering, D. J., & Pollock, J. (2001). *Classroom instruction that works: Research-based strategies for increasing student achievement.* Alexandria, VA: Association for Supervision and Curriculum Development.
Stronge, J. H. (2007). *Qualities of effective teachers* (2nd ed.). Alexandria, VA: Association for Supervision and Curriculum Development.

2 Popham, W. J. (2008). *Transformative assessment.* Alexandria, VA: Association for Supervision and Curriculum Development, pp. 137–138.

3 Popham, W. J. (2008). p. 138.

4 Adapted from: Stronge, J. H., & Tucker, P. D. (2003). *Handbook on teacher evaluation.* Larchmont, NY: Eye On Education.

5 Viadero, D. (2004, January 21). Achievement-gap study emphasizes better use of data. *Education Week*, p. 9.

6 Tucker, P. D., & Stronge, J. H. (2005). *Linking teacher evaluation and student learning.* Alexandria, VA: Association for Supervision and Curriculum Development. p. 11.

7 Little, J., Gearhart, M., Curry, M., & Kafka, J. (2003). Looking at student work for teacher learning, teacher community, and school reform. *Phi Delta Kappan, 85*(3), 185–192.

8 Little, J., Gearhart, M., Curry, M., & Kafka, J. (2003).

9 Peery, A. (2004). *Deep change: Professional development from the inside out.* Lanham, MD: Scarecrow Press.

10 Zila, R. (2005). Thompson School District, personal communication. Reported in Tucker, P. D., & Stronge, J. H. (2005), p. 52.

11 Good, T. L., & Brophy, J. E. (1997). *Looking in Classrooms* (7th ed.). New York: Addison-Wesley. p. 217.

12 Butler, R. (1988). Enhancing and undermining intrinsic motivation: The effects of task-involving and ego-involving evaluation on interest and performance. *British Journal of Educational Psychology, 58*, 1–14. (Cited in Black, Harrison, Lee, Marshall, & Wiliam, 2004).

13 Black, P., Harrison, C., Lee, C., Marshall, B., & Wiliam, D. (2004). Working inside the black box: Assessment for learning in the classroom. *Phi Delta Kappan, 86*(1), 9–21. p. 13

14 Carnoy, M., & Loeb, S. (2002). Does external accountability affect student outcomes? A cross-state analysis. *Educational Evaluation and Policy Analysis, 24*(4), 305–331. p. 305.

15 See, for example: Mendro, R. L. (1998). Student achievement and school and teacher accountability. *Journal of Personnel Evaluation in Education, 12*(3), 257–267.

16 McConney, A. A., Schalock, M. D., & Schalock, H. D. (1997). Indicators of student learning in teacher evaluation. In J. H. Stronge (Ed.), *Evaluating teaching: A guide to current thinking and best practice* (pp. 162-192). Thousand Oaks, CA: Corwin Press. p. 162.

Part II

Practice with Student Achievement Goals: Samples to Consider

Part II of this book provides examples of student achievement goal setting. Section 1 includes teacher examples from multiple subject areas and from multiple school levels, and Section 2 provides examples from the varied positions included under educational specialist. These goals were developed using the five-step process that was presented in Chapter 1 and discussed in more detail in Chapter 2. The following table provides an overview of the examples included.

Educational Professional	Position	School Level			Content/Program Area
		Elementary	Middle	High School	
Section 1: Teacher Examples					
Marilyn Thomas	Kindergarten Teacher	X			Early Literacy Skills
Delinda Groebels	Art Teacher	X			Art Skills
Thuy Nguyen	Fourth-Grade Teacher	X			Reading
Sonja Fox	Physical Education Teacher		X		Overall Fitness
Albert Findlay	Mathematics Teacher		X		Pre-Algebra
Dan Forrest	Chorus Teacher		X		Vocal Music
Donna Francis	Special Education Teacher		X		Reading
Felicia Martin	Social Studies Teacher			X	IB History
Joshua Baker	Science Teacher			X	Biology/Scientific Investigation
Section 2: Educational Specialist Examples					
Anna Foster	Library/Media Specialist	X			Reading Comprehension/Accelerated Reader Program
Jasmine Nichols	School Social Worker			X	Attendance of Pregnant High School Youths and Mothers
Bill Hayes	Guidance Counselor			X	Freshman Success
Melanie Brewster	Instructional Coach	X			Mathematics
Keisha Lyttle	Literacy Coach		X		Reading
Juan Rios	Physical Therapist	X	X	X	Correct Positioning of Students

Section 1

Sample Student Achievement Goals for Teachers

Educator's Name: <u>Marilyn Thomas</u>	
School: <u>Adams Elementary School</u> Position: <u>Kindergarten Teacher</u>	
I. Setting (Describe the population and special learning circumstances)	I teach in a rural K–5 school with 245 students. Thirty-two percent of the students in the school receive free and reduced lunch. My class has 22 children, 12 males and 10 females. One student goes to resource for reading instruction, and one student receives speech services. Four students are up for child study review for issues related to possible learning disabilities.
II. Content/Subject/ Field Area (The area/topic addressed based on learner achievement, data analysis, or observational data)	Basic early literacy skills is critical at the kindergarten level to help students learn to read.
III. Baseline Data (What do the current data show?)	In September, the Dynamic Indicators of Basic Early Literacy Skills (DIBELS) tests showed that 15 students met benchmarks on the DIBELS and are "at grade level." Six students require strategic intervention because they have not met the benchmarks in all four areas. One student requires intensive intervention as she is identified as at risk.
IV. Goal Statement (Describe what you want students to accomplish.)	For the current school year, all of my students will make measurable progress on the DIBELS assessment. The six students who require strategic intervention will be at grade level by the end of the year, and the one student who is "at risk/emerging" will move to the category of "low risk/established" on three of four areas tested by DIBELS.

V.	Strategies (Activities used to accomplish the goal)	• Attend workshop on using the Building Blocks® program: Language Concepts, Print Concepts, Phonemic Awareness, Letters and Sounds, Desire to Learn to Read and Write, Interesting Words; implement program. • Increase parental involvement in reading at home and work on early literacy skills. • Use guided reading groups to focus on specific groups of students.
VI.	Mid-Year Review (Describe goal progress and other relevant data.)	The students are making measurable progress. I administered the mid-year DIBELS and found that the 15 students who met the benchmarks in September are continuing to meet benchmarks. Of the six students who required strategic intervention, one has met the benchmarks on the four areas, and the other five still require strategic intervention. The one student who was "at-risk/emerging" has moved to "low-risk/established" on three of the four areas. I will continue to use the strategies that I implemented. Parents are sending notes indicating involvement, and students are responding to the guided reading groups.
VII.	End-of-Year Results (Accomplishments at the end of year)	Based on the end of the year DIBELS assessment, five of the six students requiring strategic intervention are now on grade level. The student who was at-risk/emerging moved to low-risk/established on four areas. Twenty of the students are now on grade level. The one student who failed to meet the benchmark is currently under child study review.

Educator's Name: Delinda Groebels	
School: Wonderland Elementary	Position: Art Teacher
I. Setting (Describe the population and special learning circumstances.)	The setting is four classes of third-grade students. There are 90 students total. Of the third graders I teach, one student is currently taking private art lessons and one student has taken private art lessons within the past two years. Forty-three third graders have been enrolled at Wonderland Elementary since kindergarten. Two students are classified as English for speakers of other languages (ESOL). All third graders receive 45 minutes of art instruction each week.
II. Content/Subject/ Field Area (The area/topic addressed based on learner achievement, data analysis, or observational data)	The district curriculum objectives addressed in art are the following: classifying materials, classifying techniques, and classifying processes.
III. Baseline Data (What do the current data show?)	Baseline data show that less than 1% of my students met the benchmark (80% score) on the art assessment developed by the district. Two students out of 90 met the benchmark. These were the two students who have been taking art lessons outside of school.
IV. Goal Statement (Describe what you want students to accomplish.)	In the current school year, all of my students will show measurable growth in the subject area of art. At least 80% of my students will meet or exceed the benchmark for the art assessment.

V. Strategies (Activities used to accomplish the goal)	• Exposure to and activities with materials, techniques, and processes • Art journal for student observations in which I will provide feedback on the application of materials, techniques, and processes • Frequent formative assessments of student work with feedback and opportunities to redo work if needed
VI. Mid-Year Review (Describe goal progress and other relevant data.)	At mid-year the students are showing progress. I administered an alternate form of the art assessment and found that 20%, or 18 students have now met the benchmark, and 48 or 53% are within 20 percentage points of meeting the benchmark. The students are having the most trouble with the third objective, classifying processes. I will incorporate teaching strategies such as concept attainment and inductive approaches to classification. We will include a classification project during the last nine weeks.
VII. End-of-Year Results (Accomplishments at the end of year)	After administering the end of year art assessment, my students have met the goal set. Ninety percent, or 81 students, met the benchmark of 80% on the assessment. Of the 9 students who failed to meet the benchmark, 4 scored in the 70s on the benchmark, and 5 had frequent absences from art because of time spent with resource teachers.

Educator's Name: Thuy Nguyen	
School: District Elementary School Position: Fourth-Grade Teacher	
I. Setting (Describe the population and special learning circumstances.)	I teach in a suburban K–5 school with 560 students. Twenty-two percent of the students in the school receive free and reduced lunch. The total number of students in my class is 19, with 10 girls and 9 boys. One student receives learning disability resources, three are in speech therapy, and two have 504 plans related to auditory processing issues.
II. Content/Subject/ Field Area (The area/topic addressed based on learner achievement, data analysis, or observational data)	Reading achievement is targeted in the school improvement plan. Last year 55% of my fourth-grade students demonstrated one year's growth on the third-grade reading test.
III. Baseline Data (What do the current data show?)	The state reading assessment has four possible levels. The baseline data show that 4 (21%) of my students are at Level 4 or higher, 10 (53%) are at Level 3, 3 (16%) are at Level 2, and 2 (10%) are at Level 1 on the state reading assessment. STAR data reveal that 58% of students are reading on or above grade level.
IV. Goal Statement (Describe what you want students to accomplish.)	For the current school year, all of my students will be reading on or above grade level by the end of the school year as measured by the STAR assessment.

V. Strategies (Activities used to accomplish the goal)	<ul><li>Attend training on the use of Reader's Workshop in class, and implement the program.</li><li>Monitor progress of students using STAR assessments.</li><li>Institute daily reading time and book discussion with students within zones of proximal development in reading.</li><li>Collaborate with reading specialist to identify specific student needs.</li></ul>
VI. Mid-Year Review (Describe goal progress and other relevant data.)	For the remainder of the year I will continue with the strategies listed, but I will differentiate Reader's Workshop to focus on specific skills for students. I will continue to work with the reading specialist to target those students who are below grade level and target instruction to focus on specific needs. According to the January STAR report, 68% of my students are reading on or above grade level.
VII. End-of-Year Results (Accomplishments at the end of year)	At the end of the year, 18 out of 19 students were reading on grade level. The one student who was not on grade level has been targeted for further intervention during the summer.

Educator's Name: <u>Sonja Fox</u>	
School: <u>Sunshine Middle School</u> Position: <u>P.E. Teacher</u>	
I. Setting (Describe the population and special learning circumstances.)	I teach in an urban middle school with 824 students. Forty-five percent of the students are on free and reduced lunch. I teach sixth-, seventh-, and eighth-grade students.
II. Content/Subject/Field Area (The area/topic addressed based on learner achievement, data analysis, or observational data)	The area I will address is student progress on the Presidential Fitness Tests. Improvement on the Presidential Fitness Tests indicates overall improvement in physical education. Presidential Fitness Test goals are based on students who score at the 85th percentile or better in each sub area. Sixth-grade students typically do not perform as well on this test.
III. Baseline Data (What do the current data show?)	A pretest of each sub area shows that a majority of my sixth-grade students failed to reach the benchmarks on the five Presidential Fitness subtests.
IV. Goal Statement (Describe what you want students to accomplish.)	In the current school year, my sixth-grade students will improve on each of the Presidential Fitness subtests by an average of 20%.
V. Strategies (Activities used to accomplish the goal)	• Have students set daily activity goals for an eight-week time period, and have them keep daily activity logs. • Test students on the Presidential Fitness subtest areas once per month. • Incorporate student goal setting by having students track their progress using graphs.

VI. Mid-Year Review (Describe goal progress and other relevant data.)	My students are making some progress. However, only 2 of them at this time have met the benchmark of 20% improvement on each of the Presidential Fitness Sub-tests. These students were almost at the benchmark when the Presidential Fitness Test was administered in August. Eight of my students have not made any improvement at all. The students used the daily activity log, but ten students did not complete it. Students are tracking their progress, but the students who are not progressing are losing interest. I will use the daily activity log during one more eight-week period and provide incentives for completing it. I will also continue with student goal setting because it helps students see their progress. However, I am going to work with each student to set smaller, incremental goals. I am also going to register to participate in the "Active Lifestyles Program" administered by the President's Challenge. Students earn points and win awards for maintaining an active lifestyle.
VII. End-of-Year Results (Accomplishments at the end of year)	At the end of the year, 70% of my students improved on their subtests by at least 20%. I am pleased with the progress as I made a stretch goal of 100%. I will continue working with these students as they progress to seventh grade to continue their improvement.

Educator's Name: <u>Albert Findlay</u>	
School: <u>Greene Middle School</u> Position: <u>Eighth-Grade Math Teacher</u>	
I. Setting (Describe the population and special learning circumstances.)	I teach four sections of pre-algebra each day to a total of 72 students—17 males and 55 females. The middle school has about 890 students in sixth through eighth grade, and it is located in an urban city. The transient rate at the school is approximately 28% with some students experiencing high mobility and homelessness.
II. Content/Subject/ Field Area (The area/topic addressed based on learner achievement, data analysis, or obser-vational data)	Our state has five main objectives for mathematics. These include problem-solving, reasoning and proofs, communication, connections, and representations. Based on student achievement data for the school, students need assistance in all five areas. However, the category of reasoning and proofs and the category of representations are the most challenging.
III. Baseline Data (What do the current data show?)	I used the mathematics textbook preassessment that is aligned to our state objectives. There were 41 questions on the test, and the results could be disaggregated by objectives. Each objective totaled 20 points on the assessment. The data revealed the following average number of points per area: Problem-solving—12 out of 20 points Reasoning—10 out of 20 points Communication—15 out of 20 points Connections—8 out of 20 points Representations—10 out of 20 points The data show that the students need to work in each area. Specific weaknesses include connections, reasoning, and representations.
IV. Goal Statement (Describe what you want students to accomplish.)	For the current school year, all students will demonstrate measurable progress in each of the five objective areas. At least 80 percent will meet the benchmark set on the overall pre-algebra assessment.

V. Strategies (Activities used to accomplish the goal)	• Incorporate SCANS skills by using numbers, fractions, and percentages to solve problems; use tables, graphs, and charts; use computers to enter, retrieve, change, and communicate numerical information. • Incorporate goal setting with students by having students track progress toward their goals. • Offer after-school tutoring two days per week to students who need help.
VI. Mid-Year Review (Describe goal progress and other relevant data.)	I attended the SCANS workshop and incorporated this approach into my lessons. I have not yet incorporated computers but will work with the instructional technology teacher to do so. Informal assessment data indicate that at least 38 of my students are continuing to struggle with mathematics concepts. I plan to meet with the mathematics coach to discuss specific needs and develop intervention plans for students. Goal setting seems to be working with many students, but some students are discouraged when they can visually see that they are not meeting their goals. I will work with students to set realistic, incremental goals. Four students left the school and three students came in during the first part of the year. I administered the preassessments to the new students to determine their needs.
VII. End-of-Year Results (Accomplishments at the end of year)	At the end of the year, 74% of my students met the benchmark on the pre-algebra postassessment. At the end of the year I had 65 students, and only 58 of the 65 students were with me throughout the year.

Educator's Name: Dan Forrest	
School: Tiger Middle School Position: Chorus Teacher	
I. Setting (Describe the population and special learning circumstances.)	I teach chorus to sixth-, seventh-, and eighth-grade students. There are approximately 900 students at this suburban middle school.
II. Content/Subject/ Field Area (The area/topic addressed based on learner achievement, data analysis, or observational data)	I will focus on sixth-grade chorus students because they are learning the most about music at the middle level. We will further focus on vocal music based on the state music standards.
III. Baseline Data (What do the current data show?)	I used the state rubrics for sight-singing composition, sight-singing performance, and group work based on a performance assessment. Based on a four-level rubric with a score of 3 as proficient, the average scores for sixth-grade choral students were as follows: Sight-singing composition—2 Sight-singing performance—2 Group work—1.5
IV. Goal Statement (Describe what you want students to accomplish.)	For the current school year, all students will demonstrate measurable progress on each of the areas noted above. The average level of performance of sixth-grade students will improve to the following levels: Sight-singing composition—3.5 Sight-singing performance—3.5 Group work—3

V. Strategies (Activities used to accomplish the goal)	• Share rubrics for the three areas with students and provide examples of student performance. • Have students apply rubrics to their own work and the work of others. • Provide multiple experiences in performing sight-singing as a class. • Provide instruction in using compositional devices, musical notations, and terms and symbols.

VI. Mid-Year Review (Describe goal progress and other relevant data.)	The students are making progress on their sight-singing examples and in working together. At mid-year I administered a performance assessment, and the average performance levels of sixth-grade students were as follows:
	    Sight-singing composition—2.5
	    Sight-singing performance—2.5
	    Group work—2
	The students are still having trouble in working together as a group. I will use cooperative learning strategies to improve group performance.

VII. End-of-Year Results (Accomplishments at the end of year)	At the end of the year, the average performance levels of sixth-grade students were:
	    Sight-singing composition—3.5
	    Sight-singing performance—3.5
	    Group work—2.5
	All students made measurable progress on each of the three areas.

Educator's Name: Donna Francis

School: Green Ridge Middle School   Position: Special Education Teacher

I. Setting (Describe the population and special learning circumstances.)	The school consists of 750 students in which 64% are on free and reduced lunch. I teach one class of 18 students for seventh-grade English/ language arts (ELA). These students are pulled out of their regular classroom for ELA. All of the students served in the learning disabilities classes are on free and reduced lunch. Two students are female and 16 students are males. There are 7 African American males, 6 white males, 3 Hispanic male, and 2 African American females.
II. Content/Subject/ Field Area (The area/topic addressed based on learner achievement, data analysis, or observational data)	Reading comprehension is the content area that will be addressed because this area was identified in each of the students' individualized education plans (IEPs).
III. Baseline Data (What do the current data show?)	The Woodcock-Johnson test was administered in August. The baseline data show that all of the students are reading below grade level. The range of grade equivalency is 1.2 to 5.7.
IV. Goal Statement (Describe what you want students to accomplish.)	For the current school year, all students will show measurable progress on the Woodcock-Johnson. The students will increase their Woodcock-Johnson score by an average of 1.5 years.

V. Strategies (Activities used to accomplish the goal)	• Receive refresher training and use prescriptive reading program. • Use the mastery measurements to record student progress. • Maintain running records to record student progress.
VI. Mid-Year Review (Describe goal progress and other relevant data.)	Based on running records and mastery measurements, students are making progress and improving in reading comprehension.
VII. End-of-Year Results (Accomplishments at the end of year)	At the end of the year, the students improved an average of 1.7 years on the Woodcock Johnson Test.

Educator's Name: <u>Felicia Martin</u> School: <u>Founding Fathers High School</u> Position: <u>IB Government Teacher</u>	
I. Setting (Describe the population and special learning circumstances.)	Urban comprehensive high school with a student population of approximately 3,600 students. The school has a large special education student and English as a second language population. The school has an International Baccalaureate (IB) magnet program so that advanced students can take college-level courses. There are 44 seniors in two sections of IB history. Fifteen are male and 29 are female. Sixteen students have limited English proficiency. Students are seniors completing the second year of a two-year program in history.
II. Content/Subject/ Field Area (The area/topic addressed based on learner achievement, data analysis, or observational data)	The course is IB History of the Americas, and the focus is the skills and knowledge defined by the IB History Subject Guide Objectives.
III. Baseline Data (What do the current data show?)	The previous year's IB history examination was administered as a pretest. The pretest shows that 2 out of 44 (4.5%) students score at a Level 4.
IV. Goal Statement (Describe what you want students to accomplish.)	For the current school year, all of my students will demonstrate measurable growth in the skills and knowledge of IB history as determined by a comparison of pretest and posttest scores. At least 70% of all students shall demonstrate the skills and knowledge sufficient to predict a "4" (passing) on the IB examination, as determined by a comparison of the pretest and posttest scores.

V. Strategies (Activities used to accomplish the goal)	• Administer pre-, mid-, and posttests using previously published IB examinations to measure student progress. • Attend IB training for History of the Americas. • Use source materials to develop critical thinking skills, and construct document-based questions. • Model essay writing, and incorporate peer editing.
VI. Mid-Year Review (Describe goal progress and other relevant data.)	At mid-year I administered a previously published IB examination. Twenty students, or 45%, scored at a Level 4. The students have made progress. Three students are having difficulty and scored at a Level 1. In addition to using the strategies above, I will begin a tutoring program after school to target students who are struggling.
VII. End-of-Year Results (Accomplishments at the end of year)	At the end of the year, 72% of my students scored at a Level 4 on the IB postexamination that I administered. I will compare these postexamination scores with actual IB scores to determine whether the previously released IB exams are predictive of future performance.

Educator's Name: Joshua Baker	
School: Isaac Newton High School Position: Science Teacher	
I. Setting (Describe the population and special learning circumstances.)	This is a rural high school in a largely migrant community. Forty-four percent of our students are children of migrant farm workers, and our school has a 32% transient rate, in part because some students leave in December to go back to their native countries. I teach two sections of biology to a total of 48 students.
II. Content/Subject/ Field Area (The area/topic addressed based on learner achievement, data analysis, or obser- vational data)	The content focus is the state's high school biology standards. Based on past observations of student performance, I expect that students will have trouble using scientific investigative skills.
III. Baseline Data (What do the current data show?)	As a pretest, the students in my biology class evaluated an experiment and I scored their perfor- mance using a four-level scientific investigation rubric in which a score of "3" signifies proficiency: Question/Hypothesis—2 Investigation Design—1.5 Methods of Data Collection—1.5 Data Analysis—1.5
IV. Goal Statement (Describe what you want students to accomplish.)	For the current school year, all of my students will make measurable progress in each of the four areas related to scientific investigation, particularly within the field of biology. The students will perform at the following level of performance based on a postperformance assessment: Question/Hypothesis—3 Investigation Design—3 Methods of Data Collection—3 Data Analysis—3

V. Strategies (Activities used to accomplish the goal)	• Conduct mini-lessons on the four areas of scientific investigation. • Analyze the science investigation rubric with students, and have them apply it to their own work as well as the work of others. • Participate in the annual science fair. • Provide opportunities for scientific investigation through the weekly use of labs.
VI. Mid-Year Review (Describe goal progress and other relevant data.)	At mid-year the students are showing progress in using scientific investigation skills. Formative assessments based on four areas of scientific investigation indicate that students are improving in each of these areas. I will also be using the resources of a nearby scientific laboratory and taking students on a field trip to show how science is used in this laboratory, with a focus on the four investigative skills.

VII. End-of-Year Results (Accomplishments at the end of year)	By the end of the year, all of the students improved in their abilities to apply the principles of scientific investigation. On a postassessment in which students actually performed a scientific investigation, the average levels of performance were as follows:
	    Question/Hypothesis—3.5
	    Investigation Design—3
	    Methods of Data Collection—3.5
	    Data Analysis—3

Section 2

Sample Student Achievement/Program Goals from Educational Specialists

Educator's Name: Anna Foster
School: Niceville Elementary School   Position: Library/Media Specialist

I. Setting (Describe the population and special learning circumstances.)	Niceville Elementary School has approximately 1,000 students, 32% of whom participate in the free and reduced lunch program. Because of budget cuts, we have lost one library aide and have less money to purchase materials for the library.
II. Content/Subject/ Field Area (The area/topic addressed based on learner achievement, data analysis, or observational data)	Students are held accountable for library skills, information literacy skills, and reading comprehension on the state assessment, and these are areas identified by our school improvement plan. Based on the Accelerated Reader (AR) scores and STAR diagnostic tests, students are weak in reading comprehension. Only sixty-five percent of third graders, 71% of fourth graders, and 68% of fifth graders passed the state reading assessment.
III. Baseline Data (What do the current data show?)	According to baseline data, only 54% of students, on average, chose a book within their zone of proximal development established by the STAR assessment, and only 60% of students who took Accelerated Reader (AR) tests obtained a passing score by answering at least 80% of questions correctly.
IV. Goal Statement (Describe what you want students to accomplish.)	For the current school year, all of my students will demonstrate measurable progress in choosing appropriate books to read and in obtaining passing scores on AR tests. At least 80% of third-, fourth-, and fifth-grade students will choose books within their zones of proximal development, and at least 80% will achieve passing scores on AR tests taken.

V.	Strategies (Activities used to accomplish the goal)	• Improve students' reading comprehension through the use of information literacy skills. • Use digital note cards to document students' work on reading passages, such as their extraction of main ideas and facts. • Monitor students' access to the AR books and software.
VI.	Mid-Year Review (Describe goal progress and other relevant data.)	By mid-year, approximately 70% of students chose books within their zones of proximal development, and 65% of students achieved pass rates of 80% on their AR tests. In addition to continuing with the strategies above, I will create mobile carts for teachers to take into their classrooms to provide students with easier access to books within their zones of proximal development.
VII.	End-of-Year Results (Accomplishments at the end of year)	At the end of the year, 84% of students chose a book within their zone of proximal development, and 75% achieved passing scores on the AR tests they took.

Educator's Name: Jasmine Nichols	
School: District position Position: School Social Worker	
I. Setting (Describe the population and special learning circumstances.)	I serve the secondary schools in a diverse district of 12,000 students.
II. Content/Subject/ Field Area (The area/topic addressed based on learner achievement, data analysis, or observational data)	The goal is to increase learner access by removing barriers for high school youth who are pregnant or have had children. Unfortunately, many high school youth drop out of school after becoming pregnant or giving birth.
III. Baseline Data (What do the current data show?)	High school mothers and pregnant youth have lower attendance rates then their same-age peers and are at a higher risk for dropping out of school. Last year, we had 32 high school mothers and pregnant youth. On average, these students missed 50% of the school year. Of the 32 students, 18 dropped out of school.
IV. Goal Statement (Describe what you want students to accomplish.)	For the current school year, high school mothers and pregnant students will miss no more than 30% of school days, and dropout rates will decrease by 50%.

V. Strategies (Activities used to accomplish the goal)	• Identify barriers to regular school attendance through focus group meetings with students. • Establish relationships with teens and parents and/or guardians, and begin referral process to community agencies for assistance with finances, childcare, insurance, etc. • Arrange homebound services for new mothers and facilitate communication with site-based teachers, guidance counselors, and school nurses.
VI. Mid-Year Review (Describe goal progress and other relevant data.)	At mid-year we had 29 high school mothers and pregnant youths. As of January 31st, these students missed an average of 20% of the year. At mid-year only three had dropped out of school, but I am continuing to work with the three to have them reestablished.
VII. End-of-Year Results (Accomplishments at the end of year)	At the end of the year we had 31 high school mothers and pregnant youths. On average, the students missed 32% of school days, and 26% had dropped out of school compared to last year when 56% dropped out of school.

Educator's Name: Bill Hayes	
School: Green River High School Position: Guidance Counselor	

I. Setting (Describe the population and special learning circumstances.)	Green River High School has a relatively low free and reduced lunch rate of 15%. Many of the 2,564 students are from fairly affluent backgrounds. I am assigned to the incoming freshman class and will follow them until they graduate. We have approximately 650 freshmen.
II. Content/Subject/ Field Area (The area/topic addressed based on learner achievement, data analysis, or observational data)	Course-passing rates of freshman are a concern. Based on information from 9th grade teachers, students are ill-prepared academically and do not perform well in classes. This is a trend that we continue to see with each incoming freshman class.
III. Baseline Data (What do the current data show?)	Last year, 176 out of 700 incoming freshman, or 25%, failed one or more courses.
IV. Goal Statement (Describe what you want students to accomplish.)	For the current school year, the percentage of students who fail one or more courses will be no more than 10%.
V. Strategies (Activities used to accomplish the goal)	<ul><li>Individually meet with students who have poor interim progress reports.</li><li>Provide a six-week study skills program for struggling learners.</li><li>Facilitate parent and/or guardian–teacher–student meetings to establish interventions, such as tutoring.</li></ul>

VI. Mid-Year Review (Describe goal progress and other relevant data.)	After the second nine-weeks progress report, 15% were failing one or more courses. Of the students who are failing one or more courses, 10 have stopped attending school. The social worker is working on locating these students. I am continuing to meet with students who are failing more than one subject and will notify teachers so that they are aware of students who are in danger of failing. Students have attended the study skills session, and these sessions provide time to discuss student progress and to work on study skills. I will also continue to send notifications of student progress to parents/guardians.
VII. End-of-Year Results (Accomplishments at the end of year)	At the end of the year, 72, or 11%, failed one or more courses, which is an improvement over last year in which 25% of students failed one or more courses.

Educator's Name: Melanie Brewster	
School: Cougar Elementary School Position: Instructional Coach	
I. Setting (Describe the population and special learning circumstances.)	Cougar Elementary is located in an urban setting and has an enrollment of 306 students in kindergarten through fifth grade with an average daily attendance of 95% and a free and reduced lunch rate of 39%.
II. Content/Subject/ Field Area (The area/topic addressed based on learner achievement, data analysis, or observational data)	The school has had low mathematics achievement. As an instructional coach I plan to implement a multi-year approach to improve student achievement. The baseline data show that 68% of fourth-grade students scored below the pass rate and 32% scored at or above the pass rate.
III. Baseline Data (What do the current data show?)	Our district uses the STAR mathematics assessment to track student progress. The STAR mathematics assessment was administered in August. The data show that 21% of the students are below the 25th percentile, 47% of the students are between the 26th and the 49th percentile, 23% are between the 50th and the 74th percentile, and 9% are above the 75th percentile.

IV. Goal Statement (Describe what you want students to accomplish.)	For the current school year, fourth-grade students' performance on the STAR assessment will be as follows:
	    < 25th percentile—5%
	    25th to 49th percentile—25%
	    50th percentile and above—70%

V. Strategies (Activities used to accomplish the goal)	• Staff development on data analysis • Implementation of the program Creating Excellence in Mathematics (CEEM) • Use of interim assessment data • Mentoring activities about using data analysis to drive instruction
VI. Mid-Year Review (Describe goal progress and other relevant data.)	The strategies are working well, and teachers are using the STAR data to make instructional decisions. I will hold a refresher data analysis workshop, and I will continue to offer and provide support to teachers through mini-workshops offered directly after various mathematics assessments are administered. I will also begin lunch talks to encourage teachers to discuss how their students are performing in mathematics. Progress is being made; the latest STAR assessment data show that 54% of fourth-grade students are scoring at the 50th percentile or above.
VII. End-of-Year Results (Accomplishments at the end of year)	At the end of the school year, 73% of my students exceeded the benchmark of 50th percentile or above on the percentile rank distribution for STAR, 21% fell within the 25th to 49th percentile, and 11% were at the 25th percentile or below.

Educator's Name: <u>Keisha Lyttle</u>	
School: <u>Lincoln Middle School</u> Position: <u>Literacy Coach</u>	
I. Setting (Describe the population and special learning circumstances.)	Lincoln Middle School has a 95% free and reduced lunch rate, and 97% of the population are minorities. Lincoln Middle School is located in an urban setting and serves 900 students.
II. Content/Subject/ Field Area (The area/topic addressed based on learner achievement, data analysis, or observational data)	I work with all content areas on reading across the curriculum. Reading improvement is included in the school improvement plan, and it needs to be stressed by all teachers whether or not they are teaching English/language arts.
III. Baseline Data (What do the current data show?)	Last year, 86% of eighth-grade students passed the state writing assessment, and only 36% of eighth-grade students passed the state reading assessment. Based on a survey of social studies, mathematics, and science teachers, only 50% use reading skills in their content areas.
IV. Goal Statement (Describe what you want students to accomplish.)	For the current school year, all teachers will use reading skills in the core content areas. Also, 60% of eighth-graders will pass the state reading assessment, which will be a 24 percentage point increase from last year.

V.	Strategies (Activities used to accomplish the goal)	• Provide mini-monthly professional development sessions where teachers will receive strategies and sample lessons as part of the regularly scheduled faculty meetings. • Observe core teachers conduct reading lessons, and provide feedback. • Co-teach and model reading strategies in lessons as appropriate. • Develop long-range instructional goals and plans with administrators. • Track student progress on district benchmark assessments.
VI.	Mid-Year Review (Describe goal progress and other relevant data.)	At mid-year, I have observed all core content area teachers as they use reading strategies. According to district benchmark assessments for the first and second nine weeks, the percentage of students receiving a passing score is 56%. I will continue with my strategies.
VII.	End-of-Year Results (Accomplishments at the end of year)	At the end of the school year, all teachers have been observed using reading skills in the core content areas, including mathematics, science, and social studies. The state reading assessment scores indicate that 62% of eighth-grade students passed the state reading assessment.

Educator's Name: Juan Rios	
School: District Level Position Position: Physical Therapist	
I. Setting (Describe the population and special learning circumstances.)	I work with all special needs learners ages 2–22 years in the district who require gross motor intervention to succeed to the best of their abilities in the education environment. I serve a total of 25 students.
II. Content/Subject/ Field Area (The area/topic addressed based on learner achievement, data analysis, or observational data)	My area of focus within physical therapy is classroom positioning. When learners are inappropriately positioned or moved, the health of students and teachers may be at risk. This could result in on-the-job injuries and staff absences. When the regular teacher or staff member is absent, learning is impacted. For the student, being in a less-than-optimal position results in decreased attention, difficulties controlling movement, and a lack of learning.
III. Baseline Data (What do the current data show?)	During the last school year, only 52% of students were positioned correctly based on classroom observations.
IV. Goal Statement (Describe what you want students to accomplish.)	In the current school year, all students will be positioned correctly during observation periods.
V. Strategies (Activities used to accomplish the goal)	• In-service training to staff/teachers on positioning and its importance • Written protocol on positioning • One-on-one follow-up consultation on positioning when concerns are noted • Site visitations to look for proper positioning

VI. Mid-Year Review (Describe goal progress and other relevant data.)	At mid-year I observed the five school sites for a total of three observations at each site. During these visits I observed that 75% of students were positioned correctly. One site seemed to have particular problems. I will provide intensive training to staff at this site and then follow up with frequent observations.
VII. End-of-Year Results (Accomplishments at the end of year)	At the end of the school year, 92% of students were positioned correctly. Although this did not meet the goal of 100%, it is a significant improvement over last year.

Part III

Annotated Bibliography Related to Student Achievement Goal Setting

Introduction

This annotated bibliography is provided for readers who would like to learn more about issues related to student achievement goal setting from selected research reported in the professional literature. The annotations are presented in a standard format for ease in referencing and using the information.

Matrix

The matrix that follows is intended as a guide to connect the annotations with key aspects or issues related to goal setting.

Matrix Goal-Setting Guide

Reference	Goal-Setting Process	Goal-Setting Results	Formative Assessment	Teacher Impact on Student Achievement	Professional Development	Data-based Instructional Decision Making
Azevedo, Ragan, Cromley, & Pritchett (2002)	●	●				
Bloom (1984)				●		
Fuchs, Deno, & Mirkin (1984)			●	●		●
Fuchs & Fuchs (2003)	●		●	●		●
Gillespie (2002)	●					
Good & Brophy (1997)	●					
Guskey (2003)			●			●
Jung & Guskey (2007)	●		●			
Langer & Colton (2005)	●		●	●	●	●
Little, Gearhart, Curry, & Kafka (2003)			●		●	
Martinez (2001)	●	●				
Marzano, Pickering, & Pollock (2001)	●	●		●		
Matterns (2005)		●				
McGregor & Elliot (2002)		●				
Safer & Fleischman (2005)			●			●
Snipe, Doolittle, & Herlihy (2002)	●	●			●	●
Stecker, Fuchs, & Fuchs (2005)	●	●	●	●		●
Tomlinson (1999)			●	●		●
Tucker & Stronge (2005)	●		●	●	●	
Walberg (1984)				●		
Yesseldyke & Bolt (2007)	●		●			●
Zimmerman, Bandura, & Matinez-Pons (1992)		●				

Annotated Bibliography

Azevedo, R., Ragan, S., Cromley, J. G., & Pritchett, S. (2003, April). *Do different goal-setting conditions facilitate students' ability to regulate their learning of complex science topics with RiverWeb?* **Paper presented at the Annual Meeting of the American Educational Research Association, Chicago, IL. [Paper]**

Keywords: goal-setting process, goal-setting results, teacher impact on student achievement

Summary: This study investigated the effect of different types of goal-setting interventions on high school students' ability to regulate their learning of complex science topics. The students worked in pairs and used a web-based simulation environment to learn about ecological systems. Sixteen 11th and 12th graders were randomly assigned to one of two goal-setting instructional conditions: teacher-set goals (TSG) and learner generated sub-goals (LGSG). In the LGSG condition, students were given four general learning goals and were allowed to set their own sub-goals, whereas in the TSG condition, each student pair followed a detailed script designed by the teacher. The student pairs used RiverWeb, a simulation instructional program, during a 3-week curriculum on water quality and land use. Pretest and posttest scores were used to assess students' learning, and transcripts of student discourse during several collaborative problem-solving episodes were also analyzed. The LGSG condition facilitated students' conceptual understanding significantly more than did the TSG condition. Students in the LGSG condition were more effective at regulating their learning process during knowledge construction activities such as setting sub-goals, retrieving prior knowledge, and engaging in adaptive help-seeking. Teachers played a crucial role for both the LGSG group and the TSG group by providing instruction, scaffolding learning, motivating students, and providing procedural assistance during the simulation.

Bloom, B. S. (1984). The 2 Sigma problem: The search for methods of group instruction as effective as one-to-one tutoring. *Educational Researcher, 13*(6), 4–16. **[Journal article]**

Keywords: formative assessment, teacher impact on student achievement

Summary: In this article, Benjamin Bloom differentiated among conventional instruction, mastery learning, and tutoring. Conventional instruction is a form of group instruction in which tests are administered periodically to determine students' marks. Mastery learning also is a form of group learning, but it is one in which "formative tests are given for purposes of feedback followed by corrective procedures and parallel formative tests to determine the extent to which the students have mastered the subject matter" (p. 4). Tutoring is one-to-one instruction in which formative assessment is used in a similar manner as in mastery learning.

Bloom summarized the research regarding alterable educational variables and more stable (or static) variables. He argued that the effect size of two or three alterable variables used together would be more than any one of them used alone. Bloom and his graduate students systematically combined mastery learning feedback-corrective procedures with other alterable variables to approach a 2.0 sigma effect size on school learning (i.e., the effect size of one-to-one tutoring). The article reported the following findings about classroom interventions combined with mastery learning:

♦ After the enhancement of initial cognitive prerequisites, student learning significantly improved. The short-term effect size was 0.7, and the long-term effect size on summative examination was 1.6.

♦ After providing equalized teacher interaction to all students, the experimental group achieved a 1.7 sigma effect size above the control group.

Fuchs, L. S., Deno, S. L., & Mirkin, P. K. (1984). The effects of frequent curriculum-based measurement and evaluation on pedagogy, student achievement, and student awareness of learning. *American Educational Research Journal, 21(2),* 449–460. [Journal article]

Keywords: formative assessment, teacher impact on student achievement, data-based instructional decision-making

Summary: This study investigated the educational effects of frequent curriculum-based measurement and evaluation. Thirty-nine special education teachers in the area of reading were randomly assigned to a repeated curriculum-based measurement/evaluation group and a conventional evaluation group, and each teacher selected three or four students for this project. Over the 18-week implementation, pedagogical decisions were surveyed twice, instructional structure was observed and measured three times, and students' knowledge about their learning was assessed during a final interview. Analyses indicated that teachers in the experimental group increased student achievement more than those in the control group. They also had more improvement in their instructional structure, their students were more conscious of learning goals and progress, and their decisions reflected greater realism about and responsiveness to student progress. Key findings included the following:

♦ Children whose teachers adopted the systematic measurement and evaluation procedures achieved better than students whose teachers used conventional monitoring methods.

♦ Teachers in the experimental group were more realistic about and responsive to student progress.

♦ The instructional structure of teachers in the experimental group demonstrated greater increases.

♦ The students in the experimental group were more knowledgeable about their own learning.

Fuchs, L.S., & Fuchs, D. (2003). *What is scientifically-based research on progress monitoring?* **Washington, DC: National Center on Student Progress Monitoring. [Report]**

Keywords: goal-setting process, goal-setting results, formative assessment, teacher impact on student achievement, data-based instructional decision-making

Summary: Progress monitoring helps teachers assess students' academic performance and track their progress on a regular basis, such as weekly or monthly. This document described progress-monitoring procedures implemented in the areas of reading, mathematics, spelling, and writing at the elementary grades. The report also examined selected empirical studies published on curriculum-based measurement (CBM). An overview revealed the following:

- ◆ Systematic progress monitoring could be used to enhance teacher concern about student progress and could identify students in need of additional or different forms of instruction.

- ◆ Graphed analysis of overall CBM scores could monitor the adequacy of student progress and determine when instructional modifications are necessary. CBM progress monitoring also could help teachers set meaningful student achievement goals and make sound instructional decisions.

- ◆ When CBM is combined with goal-raising, student-learning profiles, and appropriate instructional modifications, it could help teachers build stronger instructional programs that are more varied and more responsive to students' learning needs, and it could help effect better academic performance for students.

Gillespie, M. K. (2002). *EFF Research Principle: A Purposeful and Transparent Approach to Teaching and Learning. EFF Research to Practice Note.* **Washington, DC: National Institute for Literacy. [Report]**

Keywords: goal-setting process

Summary: Equipped for the Future (EFF) is a program established by the National Institute for Literacy. It is a national standards-based educational improvement initiative for basic adult education and English language learning. EFF's central objective is a purposeful and transparent approach to learning, which advocates intentionality, explicitness, and transparency in the learning environment. Teaching and learning experiences should be structured around the goals and purposes.

This report summarized research that supports a purposeful and transparent approach to learning. The findings include the following:

- ◆ "Learning is a purposeful, goal-directed activity. An ongoing goal-setting process is integral to effective learning" (p. 1).

- "Purposeful and transparent learning builds on learners' prior knowledge and experiences to construct new knowledge. Once learners' goals have been established, they begin a process of self-assessment" (p. 1).

- "Purposeful and transparent learning means that learners monitor and assess their own progress. Metacognitive strategies help them to be mindful of what is being learnt and what good performance looks like" (p. 1).

The second part of the report presented three examples of program practices that support purposeful teaching and learning. Respectively, they illustrated how students use the EFF framework to clarify their learning purposes, identify strengths and gaps in skills and knowledge, and make decisions to accomplish their purposes and goals.

Good, T. L., & Brophy, J. E. (1997). *Looking in classrooms* **(7th ed.). New York: Addison-Wesley. [Book]**

Keywords: goal-setting process

Summary: "Research indicates that setting goals and making a commitment to trying to reach these goals increases performance" (p. 217). The authors found that goal setting is especially effective under the following conditions:

- The goals are proximal rather than distal. The goals should be oriented to the present task rather than to some ultimate goal for the distant future. However, it is important to make students conscious of the connection between here-and-now tasks and the accomplishment of ultimate goals.

- The goals are specific rather than global.

- The goals are challenging, that is, difficult but reachable rather than too easy or too hard, and are located in the learner's zone of proximal development.

"Goal setting must be accompanied by goal commitment. Students must take the goals seriously and commit themselves to trying to reach them" (p. 217). The authors suggested that it may be beneficial to have some goal setting negotiation with students and construct student-participatory goals. The authors also proposed two ways to accomplish this. One way is to list optional goals and encourage students to take their individual potential into consideration and choose an appropriate subset. Another is performance contracting in which students are rewarded a specified grade if they achieve specified objectives. The disadvantage of this method is that it may stimulate students' extrinsic motivation instead of intrinsic motivation.

Guskey, T. R. (2003). How classroom assessments improve learning. *Educational Leadership, 60*(5), 7–12. [Journal article]

Keywords: formative assessment, data-based instructional decision-making

Summary: The article suggested that the assessments that are most conducive to improvements in student learning include quizzes, tests, and writing assignments that teachers administer on a regular basis in their classrooms, rather than the large-scale assessments designed to rank schools and students. The author argued that to achieve optimal results from classroom assessment, teachers must change both their view of assessment and their interpretation of results. Specifically, they need to view their assessments as an integral part of the instructional process and as crucial for helping students learn. Guskey suggested that to use assessments to improve instruction and student learning, teachers need to change their approach to assessment in the following three ways:

♦ Make assessments useful. The assessments should serve as meaningful sources of information for both students and teachers. They are supposed to reflect the concepts and skills that the teacher emphasizes in class, along with the teacher's criteria for judging students' performance. Students should regard them as fair measures of important learning goals. Teachers should use them to identify what they taught well and what they need to work on.

♦ Follow assessments with corrective instruction. Teachers must follow their assessments with instructional alternatives that present the concepts in new ways and engage students in different and more appropriate learning experiences.

♦ Give second chances to demonstrate success. Assessments cannot be a "one-shot, do-or-die" experience for students. They must be part of an ongoing effort to help students learn. Students should have a second chance to demonstrate their new level of competence and understanding. This second chance helps determine the effectiveness of the corrective instruction and offers students another opportunity to experience success in learning.

Jung, L. A., & Guskey, T. R. (2007). Standards-based grading and reporting: A model for special education. *Teaching Exceptional Children, 40*(2), 48–53. [Journal article]

Keywords: goal-setting process, formative assessment

Summary: A standards-based learning environment poses challenges to grading and reporting on the performances of students with disabilities who are included in general education classes. On the one hand, the general education teacher has a responsibility to grade the overall academic achievement of students on report cards; on the other hand, the special education teacher is obliged to report students' progress to individualized education plan (IEP) goals. The authors argued that more guidance and direction on developing appropriate grading policies and practices are needed. The literature revealed that teachers should individualize grading and reporting systems for students with disabilities, give more detailed descriptions of students' performance on discrete skills, and separate product, process, and progress learning goals. The authors proposed a five-step inclusive grading model:

1. Determine whether accommodations of the grade-level standards or modifications of the general curriculum are needed
2. Establish standards for modified areas
3. Determine the need for additional goals
4. Apply fair and equitable grading practices to appropriate standards
5. Communicate the meaning of the grades

Langer, G. M., & Colton, A. B. (2005). Looking at student work. *Educational Leadership, 62*(5), 22–27. **[Journal article]**

Keywords: goal-setting process, formative assessment, teacher impact on student achievement, professional development, data-based instructional decision-making

Summary: Collaborative analysis of student learning (CASL) is a certain kind of learning community in which teachers are engaged in collaborative inquiry to examine the relationship between their instruction and student performance on classroom assessments or other data that reveal information about student learning. The inquiry circle involves four steps:

1. Observe students' classroom performance, assignments, and the results of classroom assessments or standardized tests, as well as the mismatch between students' achievement versus their expected achievement
2. Analyze/interpret student work by generating several possible explanations, and invite contributions from other teachers
3. Plan the problem-solving strategies that will be implemented
4. Act on these plans

The author also argued that collaborative analysis is most powerful under the following conditions: teachers observe learners' progress over time, a theoretical framework guides the inquiry process, teachers learn and follow collaborative norms, and leadership supports the inquiry. Teachers are encouraged to learn to collaborate to explore multiple perspectives and transcend their personal limited knowledge base. School administrators and teacher leaders are encouraged to develop a shared vision for their organization and to set up an atmosphere where teachers engage in professional discussions.

The authors wrote that CASL has the potential to transform teaching, student learning, and schools in the following ways:

- ◆ It enables teachers to study how students gradually learn complex concepts and skills over time.

- ◆ CASL helps teachers understand their role in promoting students' learning.

- ◆ It helps teachers discover gaps in their own knowledge base when their instructional strategies fail, and it helps teachers enrich their knowledge base through collaboration with colleagues and specialists.

- ◆ CASL encourages school policies and practices that support learning at all levels, and it helps schools develop a positive culture in which teachers can engage in professional discussions.

Little, J., Gearhart, M., Curry, M., & Kafka, J. (2003). Looking at student work for teacher learning, teacher community, and school reform. *Phi Delta Kappan, 85*(3), 185–192. **[Journal article]**

Keywords: formative assessment, professional development

Summary: Teachers usually examine student work on their own and in isolation from colleagues. In recent years, reform advocates and professional developers have begun bringing teachers together to look at student work collaboratively. The authors conducted case studies to examine teacher groups in four school sites affiliated with three nationally recognized educational projects. The purpose of the study was to identify specific practices of collaborative efforts to look at student work and also to examine the dilemmas that teachers confront in reviewing student work. The authors found that looking at student work collaboratively could not only evaluate teachers' instruction, but it also could foster teacher learning, professional community development, and school-based reform. All projects and sites in the study shared some common elements in terms of their practices for looking at student work:

- ◆ They brought teachers together to focus on student learning and teaching practice.

- ◆ They got student work onto the table and into the conversation.

- ◆ They structured the conversation when reviewing student work.

They also observed that some practices and conditions, such as introducing protocols to guide the conversation, helped teachers to focus attention on student work and deepen their discussion. Finally, the authors explained teachers' dilemmas when examining student work collaboratively. Challenges faced included finding time to meet in collaborative groups, maintaining collegial relationships during the review, and providing clarity on what to examine in student work.

Martinez, P. (2001). *Great expectations: Setting targets for students. The Agency Reports.* **London: Learning and Skills Development Agency. [Report]**

Keywords: goal-setting process, goal-setting results, teacher impact on student achievement

Summary: This report reviewed the process of setting targets for learners. It aimed to encourage the wider use of target setting for individual students and trainees in the learning and skills sector. Section 1 addressed what types of targets should be set for individual students. The targets should be specific, challenging, achievable, and measurable. Additionally, targets should be negotiated between the teacher and the student so that the student feels ownership in the process. Section 2 offered a rationale for setting targets. The following features of target setting are supported by educational research: intervention, feedback, high expectations, and use of formative assessment. Section 3 focused on which types of learners benefit the most from targets. Section 4 discussed three models available for target setting: quantitative, qualitative, and combined (implicit and integrated). Section 5 addressed which approach is best for which learners and concluded that different approaches are appropriate depending on students' prior performance. Section 6 described key features of effective target setting: implementation, learner motivation, teaching and tutoring, management, quantitative approaches, and qualitative and combined approaches, with each one containing a list of sub-features.

Marzano, R. J., Pickering, D. J., & Pollock, J. E. (2001). *Classroom instruction that works: Research-based strategies for increasing student achievement.* **Alexandria, VA: Association for Supervision and Curriculum Development. [Book]**

Keywords: goal-setting process, goal-setting results

Summary: In Chapter 8, Setting Objectives and Providing Feedback, the authors reported findings from selected studies that synthesize research results on goal setting. The effect sizes of goal setting range from .46 to 1.37, and percentile gains range from 18 to 41. Additionally, the author examined the research results of goal setting and drew three generalizations:

- Instructional goals narrow what students focus on, and thus goal setting may have a negative effect because it focuses students' attention to such a degree that they exclude information not specifically defined in the goal.

- Instructional goals should not be too specific. Goals should be general enough to "accommodate the individual and constructivist nature of the learning process" (p. 940).

♦ Students should be encouraged to personalize teachers' goals by adapting those goals to their personal needs and desires.

The authors suggested that in classroom settings instructional goals should be specific but general enough to provide students with some flexibility to personalize those goals. The authors also said that learning contracts may be effective in developing student control of goals and ensuring students' accountability for learning outcomes. For example, a contract could be an agreement between students and teacher for a grade the students will receive if they meet established criteria.

Matterns, R. A. (2005). College students' goal orientations and achievements. *International Journal of Teaching and Learning in Higher Education, 17*(1), 27–32. **[Journal article]**

Keywords: goal-setting results

Summary: Researchers studied the relationship between type of goal orientation and academic achievement for undergraduate students enrolled in a human development course. Two types of goal orientation are mastery goals and performance goals. A review of relevant literature found that students with a high mastery orientation pursue challenges and work toward achievement of new knowledge and skills. When these students fail in some way they see the failure as a lack of effort rather than a lack of ability. Conversely, students with performance goal orientation see the ability to master goals as a statement of their own abilities and seek to maintain a positive self-image. In this study, the students completed a questionnaire and researchers found that approximately one-quarter of them had multiple goal orientations, including both mastery goals and performance goals. Approximately one-quarter had a high mastery goal orientation, and approximately one-quarter had a high performance goal orientation. Researchers found that students with multiple goal orientations did not perform significantly better in the course than did students with only high mastery or only high performance goal orientation. Students who adopted a high mastery goal orientation performed better in the course than did students with high performance goal orientation. The researchers concluded that students benefit more academically from mastery goals.

McGregor, H. A., & Elliot, A. J. (2002). Achievement goals as predictors of achievement-relevant processes prior to task engagement. *Journal of Educational Psychology, 94*(2), 381–395. **[Journal article]**

Keywords: goal-setting results

Summary: This research report comprised three studies designed to investigate mastery, performance-approach, and performance-avoidance goals as predictors of achievement-relevant processes prior to the undergraduate examination experience. All three studies involved undergraduate students enrolled in an introductory psychology class. Performance-approach goals focus on the attainment of competence relative to others, and performance-avoidance goals focus on the avoidance of incompetence relative to others. In contrast, mastery goals focus on the development of competence through task mastery. Results from across the three studies supported the authors' hypotheses and revealed a differential predictive pattern for each of the achievement goals. Mastery goals were linked to numerous positive processes, including challenge appraisals, absorption of learning materials, a lack of perceived control, calmness during the exam, preparedness, and time spent on preparation in advance of exam. Mastery goals were negative predictors of the desire to escape the exam. Performance-approach goals were linked to a more limited set of achievement-relevant variables (e.g., challenge appraisals, grade aspirations, calmness because of preparation, time spent in exam preparation), but this approach was also related to several negative processes, such as threat appraisals. Performance-avoidance goals consistently were linked to numerous negative processes (e.g., threat appraisals, anticipatory test anxiety, perceived controlledness, procrastination, low ability-related self-esteem, and lack of preparation).

Safer, N., & Fleischman, S. (2005). Research matters: How student progress monitoring improves instruction. *Educational Leadership, 62*(5), 81–83. [Journal article]

Keywords: formative assessment, data-based instructional decision-making

Summary: Student progress monitoring is a practice that helps teachers use student performance data to continuously evaluate the effectiveness of their teaching and make more informed instructional decisions. To implement student progress monitoring, the teacher first preassesses a student's current competency level on skills covered by the curriculum, sets up ultimate achievement goals for the school year, and establishes the rate of progress the student must make to attain those goals. Then the teacher uses some ongoing, frequent, "brief and easily administered measures" to monitor the student's academic progress.

Student progress monitoring is designed to assess students' growth in learning and teachers' effectiveness in teaching. Additionally, student progress monitoring can tell teachers whether the student is learning at a pace that will allow him or her to meet annual learning goals. Student progress monitoring could continually provide teachers with data and evidence about students' performance to evaluate the effectiveness of their instruction and make adjustments in their instructional decision-making.

The article's literature review revealed that student progress monitoring can help students learn more, enhance teachers' abilities in decision-making, and develop students' awareness of their own learning. Student progress monitoring is reliable and valid not only in assessing the progress of special education students, but also in evaluating the progress of English language learners and general education students who are at risk for academic failure. The authors used a detailed example to demonstrate how student progress monitoring can fit into the routine of the class-room and generate positive learning results.

Snipe, J., Doolittle, F., & Herlihy, C. (2002). *Foundations for success: Case studies of how urban school systems improve student achievement.* **New York: Manpower Demonstration Research Corporation. [Report]**

Keywords: goal-setting process, goal-setting results, professional development, data-based instructional decision-making

Summary: This report focused on the potential role of the school district as an initiator and a sustainer of academic improvement rather than a barrier to reform or a passive observer of state/school-site reforms. In the report, the Council of the Great City Schools (CGCS) and the Manpower Demonstration Research Corporation (MDRC) collaborated to conduct a long-term case study of three large urban school districts that have improved student academic achievement for their district as a whole, while also narrowing differences among racial groups. They also compared the case study districts with other districts that have not generated similar student achievement gains. The findings of the report revealed the following:

- Both the case study districts and the comparison districts faced a common set of challenges: unsatisfactory academic achievement, political conflict, inexperienced teaching staff, low expectations, a lack of demanding curriculum, a lack of instructional coherence, high student mobility, and unsatisfactory business operations.

- In the case study school districts, the leaders created important political and organizational preconditions for reform (e.g., creating a new role for the school board, developing a shared vision among key stake-holders, diagnosing the local educational situation, etc.).

- These three school districts under study had several strategies in common which they adopted to improve student achievement:

- They enthusiastically embraced state accountability systems and created a goal-focused culture. They targeted student academic performance, made efforts to clarify specific student achievement goals, set schedules with defined consequences, aligned curricula with state standards, and helped translate these standards into instructional practice.

- These school districts created concrete accountability systems that went beyond what the states had established to hold district leadership and building-level staff personally responsible for producing results.

- They focused on the lowest-performing schools.

♦ They adopted or developed district-wide curricula and instructional approaches rather than allowing each school to devise their own strategies.

♦ These school districts developed uniform elementary and middle school curricula and instructional approaches that were supported by the central office through professional development and were implemented consistently throughout the district, instead of allowing each school to devise its own curricula.

♦ They committed themselves to data-driven decision-making and instruction. These school districts gave early and ongoing assessment data to teachers and principals and also trained and supported them as the data were used to diagnose teacher and student weaknesses and modify classroom instructional practices. Central office staff, administrators, and teachers in the case study districts made a concerted effort to collect and analyze data on student performance. Formative and ongoing assessments were given to keep track of student progress, identify problems, and guide teachers' instruction. The ongoing performance measurements were for diagnostic purposes as well as for holding schools, teachers, and students accountable for the learning outcomes.

The comparison districts had several significant differences from the case study districts:

♦ They had no clear consensus among key stakeholders about priorities or an overall strategy for reform.

♦ They lacked specific, clear standards, achievement goals, timelines, and consequences.

♦ The districts' central offices took little or no responsibility for improving instruction or creating cohesive instructional strategies throughout the districts.

♦ The policies and practices of the central office were not strongly connected to intended changes in teaching and learning in the classrooms.

♦ Multiple and conflicting curricula and instructional expectations existed in these districts.

Stecker, P. M., Fuchs, L. S., & Fuchs, D. (2005). Using curriculum-based measurement to improve student achievement: Review of research. *Psychology in the Schools, 42*(8), 795–819. [Journal article]

Keywords: goal-setting process, goal-setting results, formative assessment, teacher impact on student achievement, data-based instructional decision-making

Summary: This review examined the efficacy of curriculum-based measurement (CBM) as an assessment methodology for enhancing student achievement. The authors described three distinguishing features of CBM. First, CBM assesses student progress toward long-term goals, and thus is general in nature. Second, student progress is frequently monitored (once or twice per week), and progress is graphed. Finally, CBM has a high degree of validity and reliability. The authors further described empirical studies in reading and mathematics in which teachers used CBM to monitor student progress and to make instructional decisions. Across the studies that investigated the effects of CBM on the achievement of students with disabilities, the authors drew five conclusions:

- Teachers effected significant growth with CBM if they modified instruction based on progress monitoring data. However, frequent progress monitoring alone did not boost student achievement.

- The use of data-based decision rules for interpreting graphed CBM data appeared to enable teachers to be responsive to student needs and to make appropriate instructional modifications.

- Computer applications facilitated the use of decision rules and included a goal-raising feature that also stimulated student growth.

- Skill analysis was used to categorize copious amounts of student performance information into meaningful groups of skills, and this helped teachers focus on specific students' strengths and weaknesses.

- Teachers needed consultation or instructional recommendations for using CBM information to tailor programs to meet student needs.

In general, teachers who used class-wide CBM data and peer-assisted learning strategies effected greater achievement gains among their students than did comparison teachers who used their own methods for progress monitoring and instruction.

Tomlinson, C. A. (1999). *The differentiated classroom: Responding to the needs of all learners.* **Alexandria, VA: Association for Supervision and Curriculum Development. [Book]**

Keywords: formative assessment, data-based instructional decision-making

Summary: Tomlinson proposed that in differentiated classrooms, assessment and instruction are inseparable. "In a differentiated classroom, assessment is ongoing and diagnostic" (p. 10). The goals of assessments are to provide teachers with day-to-day data on students' mental preparedness for certain learning targets and to facilitate teachers in making data-based decisions on instruction modification. The data can come from small-group discussion with the teacher and a few students, whole-class discussion, journal entries, portfolio entries, exit cards, skill inventories, pretests, homework assignments, student opinion, or interest surveys.

The primary concern of such formative assessment is to formally record students' growth, rather than to catalog students' mistakes as summative assessments would do.

Tucker, P. D., & Stronge, J. H. (2005). *Linking teacher evaluation and student learning.* **Alexandria, VA: Association for Supervision and Curriculum Development. [Book]**

Keywords: goal-setting process, formative assessment, teacher impact on student achievement, professional development

Summary: In Chapter 5, the authors examined the Performance Evaluation Program (PEP), which is a comprehensive teacher evaluation system implemented in the Alexandria City Public Schools (Virginia). This evaluation system was designed to provide greater teacher and student accountability through the connection of teacher evaluation and professional development with student goal achievement. The author defined teacher performance responsibilities in the following five general domains: instruction, assessment, learning environment, professionalism, and communications and community relations. Evaluators retrieved data from five main data sources to provide accurate feedback on teacher performance: formal observation, informal observation, portfolios, goal-setting, and student achievement. The authors stressed four purposes of student achievement goal setting:

- ◆ To establish a positive correlation between the quality of teaching and learning

- ◆ To make instructional decisions based on student data

- ◆ To create a mechanism for school improvement

- ◆ To increase effectiveness of instruction through continuous professional growth

Teachers collaborated with administrators and PEP specialists to collect and analyze data to develop annual goals that were specific, measurable, attainable, realistic, and time bound. Teachers were encouraged to customize the annual goals for personal use. Ideally, an annual goal should contain the following factors:

- ◆ Demographic information about the teacher (e.g., content area, grade level, school, etc.)

- ◆ Baseline information about the students (e.g., pretest scores, attendance records standardized test scores, status as gifted or at risk, etc.)

- ◆ Goal statement describing desired results

- ◆ Strategies that have been selected to accomplish the goal

- ◆ Progress report at mid-year or at other appropriate intervals

- ◆ Summary of end-of-year accomplishments

The authors conducted a series of interviews with administrators, teachers, and PEP specialists. Advantages of PEP are that it encourages teacher reflection and date-driven decision making, fosters teacher collaboration and collegiality, enables teachers to be active participants in their evaluation, and emphasizes formative as well as summative evaluation. Disadvantages of PEP are that it can be time-consuming, student data may be misused or misinterpreted, and evaluating teachers based on student academic progress can be perceived as threatening.

Walberg, H. J. (1984). Improving the productivity of America's schools. *Educational Leadership, 41(8), 19–27.* **[Journal article]**

Keywords: teacher impact on student achievement

Summary: During his career, Walberg tried to develop a comprehensive framework for the analysis of productivity and test it in a variety of classroom studies in the United States and other countries. In this article, the author estimated the magnitude of causal effects of education inputs on outputs. He proposed nine factors that might have a cause-and-effect relationship on students' affective, behavioral, and cognitive learning. Respectively, they are ability/prior achievement, development, motivation, amount of student time-on-task, quality of instruction, home environment, classroom social group, peer group, and use of out-of-school time. The author argued that manipulating these more direct and alterable factors promises more opportunity to improve educational productivity than focusing on less alterable variables, such as financial expenditures per student by school and school district, political decision-making, and socioeconomic status of students. Additionally, these nine factors can meet three principles of the scientific canon—parsimony, replication, and generalizability.

After exhaustive analysis and synthesis of nearly 3,000 research studies, the author reported the following:

- ◆ These nine productive factors are the chief influences on cognitive, affective, and behavioral learning. Many aspects of these factors can be altered or influenced by educators.

- ◆ Student aptitude (IQ) is a strong correlate of general academic learning but only a moderate one of science learning.

- ◆ Motivation and self-concept are weaker correlates of student learning.

- ◆ Good quality of instruction could positively affect student achievement. Among the factors of instructional quality, reinforcement has an effect size (ES) of 1.17 on educational outcomes. The effect of cues, engagement, and corrective feedback is approximately one standard deviation. Personalized and adaptive instruction, tutoring, and diagnostic- prescriptive methods also have strong effects on student learning; their effect sizes are 0.57, 0.45, 0.40, and 0.33, respectively.

- ◆ The effects of high teacher expectations, reduced class size, and computer-assisted instruction are quite small.

- ◆ Instructional time has a correlation of 0.38 with learning outcomes.

- ◆ Graded homework (ES = 0.79), class morale (ES = 0.60), school-parent programs (ES = 0.50), and home environment (ES = 0.37) have strong predictive powers on student learning.

- ◆ The influences of assigned homework, socioeconomic status, and peer groups are moderate.

- ◆ Autonomous learning/open education, which is more focused on nonachievement goals, such as attitude, self-concept, and lifelong learning, makes no statistical difference on student achievement and may even sacrifice performance on standardized tests.

Yesseldyke, J., & Bolt, D. M. (2007). Effect of technology-enhanced continuous progress monitoring on math achievement. *School Psychology Review, 36*(3), 453–467. **[Journal article]**

Keywords: goal-setting process, goal-setting results, formative assessment, teacher impact on student achievement, data-based instructional decision-making

Summary: This study examined the extent to which use of a technology-enhanced continuous progress monitoring and instructional management system would enhance the results of math instruction. Eighty classrooms were selected from eight schools in seven school districts in seven states. Forty-one classrooms were randomly assigned to experimental conditions, and 39 were assigned to control conditions. This study also investigated the reliability (integrity/fidelity) in teacher implementation of the program in the classroom, and compared math results in classrooms in which teachers did and did not use the system. Teachers whose students were included in the experimental group increased practice time, matched student skill with instruction, provided feedback to students, worked to help students personalize goals, and used technology to store and analyze student progress data. Participating students were pre- and posttested using two standardized, nationally normed tests of math achievement. Results revealed that students whose teachers use continuous progress monitoring and instructional management programs significantly outperformed the students in control conditions. There was, however, considerable variability of implementation among teachers. When teachers implemented the continuous progress monitoring system with high integrity, and when they used the data from the system to manage and differentiate instruction, students gained significantly more in math than those for whom implementation was limited or nonexistent.

Zimmerman, B. J., Bandura, A., & Matinez-Pons, M. (1992). Self-motivation for academic attainment: The role of self-efficacy beliefs and personal goal setting. *American Educational Research Journal, 29*(3), 663–676. [Journal article]

Keywords: goal-setting results

Summary: This study examined the relationships among students' perceived self-efficacy, goal setting, and final course grades in high school social studies. Students' perceived self-efficacy for self-regulatory learning, students' perceived self-efficacy for academic achievement, parental goal setting, and student goal setting served as predictors of students' final course grades in social studies. The results showed that students' perceived self-efficacy and students' goals in combination accounted for 31% of the variance in students' academic course attainment. Students' beliefs about their efficacy in self-regulated learning impacted their perceived self-efficacy for academic achievement, which in turn influenced the academic goals they set for themselves and their ultimate academic attainment. The combined direct and indirect causal effect of students' perceived self-efficacy for academic achievement on their final grades of social studies was $p = 0.37$. The students' personal grade goals were moderately correlated to their final grade. Students' prior grades were predictive of their parents' grade goals for them, which in turn were causally related to the grade goals that students set for themselves. In short, students' beliefs that they could, indeed, perform well in social studies were related to how well they performed and the types of personal goals they set for themselves.

References

Azevedo, R., Ragan, S., Cromley, J. G., & Pritchett, S. (2003, April). *Do different goal-setting conditions facilitate students' ability to regulate their learning of complex science topics with RiverWeb?* Paper presented at the Annual Meeting of the American Educational Research Association, Chicago, IL.

Bambrick-Santoyo, P. (2008). Data in the driver's seat. *Educational Leadership, 65*(4), 43–47.

Barton, P. E. (2003). *Parsing the achievement gap: Baselines for tracking student progress.* Princeton, NJ: Educational Testing Service.

Black, P., Harrison, C., Lee, C., Marshall, B., & Wiliam, D. (2004). Working inside the black box: Assessment for learning in the classroom. *Phi Delta Kappan, 86,* 9–21.

Black, P. & Wiliam, D. (1998). Inside the black box: Raising standards through classroom assessment. *Phi Delta Kappan, 80,* 139–148.

Bloom, B. S. (1984). The search for methods of group instruction as effective as one-to-one tutoring. *Educational Leadership, 41*(8), 4–17.

Bloom, B. S. (1984). The 2 Sigma problem: The search for methods of group instruction as effective as one-to-one tutoring. *Educational Researcher, 13*(6), 4–16.

Butler, R. (1988). Enhancing and undermining intrinsic motivation: The effects of task-involving and ego-involving evaluation on interest and performance. *British Journal of Educational Psychology, 58,* 1–14.

Carnoy, M., & Loeb, S. (2002). Does external accountability affect student outcomes? A cross-state analysis. *Educational Evaluation and Policy Analysis, 24,* 305–331.

Cawelti, G. (Ed.). (2004). *Handbook of research on improving student achievement* (2nd ed.). Arlington, VA: Educational Research Service.

Covino, E. A., & Iwanicki, E. (1996). Experienced teachers: Their constructs on effective teaching. *Journal of Personnel Evaluation in Education, 11,* 325–363.

Dunkin, M. J. (1978). Student characteristics, classroom processes, and student achievement. *Journal of Educational Psychology, 70,* 998–1009.

Dunkin, M. J., & Doenau, S. J. (1980). A replication study of unique and joint contributions to variance in student achievement. *Journal of Educational Psychology, 72,* 394–403.

Education Week. (2008). *Standards, assessment, and accountability. Quality counts 2008.* Retrieved May 1, 2008, from http://www.edweek.org/media/ew/qc/2008/18sos.h27.saa.pdf.

Florida Department of Education (n.d.). *Assessment and school performance: Frequently asked questions.* Retrieved May 20, 2008, from http://www.fldoe.org/faq/default.asp?Dept=179&ID=985#Q985.

Fuchs, L. S., Deno, S. L., & Mirkin, P. K. (1984). The effects of frequent curriculum-based measurement and evaluation on pedagogy, student achievement, and student awareness of learning. *American Educational Research Journal, 21*(2), 449–460.

Fuchs, L. S., & Fuchs, D. (2003). *What is scientifically-based research on progress monitoring?* Washington, DC: National Center on Student Progress Monitoring.

Gall, M. D., Gall, J. P., & Borg, W. R. (2003). *Educational research: An introduction* (7th ed.). New York: Allyn & Bacon.

Gareis C. R., & Grant, L. W. (2008). *Teacher-made assessments: How to connect curriculum, instruction, and student learning.* Larchmont, NY: Eye On Education.

Gillespie, M. K. (2002). *EFF research principle: A purposeful and transparent approach to teaching and learning. EFF research to practice note.* Washington, DC: National Institute for Literacy.

Good, T. L., & Brophy, J. E. (1997). *Looking in classrooms* (7th ed.). New York: Addison-Wesley.

Gwinnett County Public Schools. (n.d.). *Academic knowledge and skills assessment program.* Retrieved May 20, 2008, from http://gwinnett.k12.ga.us/gcps-instruction01.nsf/ImagesNavigators/F8080CC5B1B91339852571C70065213E/$file/2006–07Grade8promotion.pdf.

Guskey, T. R. (2003). How classroom assessments improve learning. *Educational Leadership, 60*(5), 6–11.

Hargreaves, E. (2005). Assessment for learning? Thinking outside the (black) box. *Cambridge Journal of Education, 35*(2), 213–224.

Heffernan, L. (2004). *Critical literacy and writer's workshop.* Newark, DE: International Reading Association.

Individuals with Disabilities Education Act. (2004). 20 U.S.C. §1401 et seq., 34 C.F.R. §300.320.

Jung, L. A., & Guskey, T. R. (2007). Standards-based grading and reporting: A model for special education. *Teaching Exceptional Children, 40*(2), 48–53.

Lachat, M. A., & Smith, S. (2005). Practices that support data use in urban high schools. *Journal of Education for Students Placed At Risk, 10*(3), 333–349.

Lance, K. C. (2004). Libraries and student achievement. The importance of school libraries for improving student achievement. *Threshold,* 8–9. Retrieved May 1, 2008, from http://www.ciconline.org.

Langer, G. M., & Colton A. B. (2005). Looking at student work. *Educational Leadership, 62*(5), 22–27.

Little, J., Gearhart, M., Curry, M., & Kafka, J. (2003). Looking at student work for teacher learning, teacher community, and school reform. *Phi Delta Kappan, 85*(3), 185–192.

Locke, E., & Latham, G. (1990). *A theory of goal setting and task performance.* Englewood Cliffs, NJ: Prentice-Hall.

Margolis, H. (2007). Monitoring your child's IEP: A focus on reading. *Insights on Learning Disabilities, 4*(2), 1–25.

Maryland Department of Education (n.d.). *High school assessment. Testing.* Retrieved May 20, 2008, from http://www.marylandpublicschools. org/MSDE/testing/hsa/.

Martinez, P. (2001). *Great expectations: Setting targets for students. The Agency Reports.* London: Learning and Skills Development Agency.

Marzano, R. J., Pickering, D. J., & Pollock, J. E. (2001). *Classroom instruction that works: Research-based strategies for increasing student achievement.* Alexandria, VA: Association for Supervision and Curriculum Development.

Matterns, R. A. (2005). College students' goal orientations and achievements. *International Journal of Teaching and Learning in Higher Education, 17*(1), 27–32.

McConney, A. A., Schalock, M. D., & Schalock, H. D. (1997). Indicators of student learning in teacher evaluation. In J. H. Stronge (Ed.), *Evaluating teaching: A guide to current thinking and best practice* (pp. 162–192). Thousand Oaks, CA: Corwin Press.

McGregor, H. A., & Elliot, A. J. (2002). Achievement goals as predictors of achievement-relevant processes prior to task engagement. *Journal of Educational Psychology, 94*(2), 381–395.

Mendro, R. L. (1998). Student achievement and school and teacher accountability. *Journal of Personnel Evaluation in Education, 12*, 257–267.

Noonan, B., & Duncan, C. R. (2005). Peer and self-assessment in high schools. *Practical Assessment, Research, and Evaluation, 10*(17), 1–8.

Ornstein, A. C., & Hunkins, F. P. (1998). *Curriculum: Foundations, principles, and issues* (3rd ed.). Boston: Allyn and Bacon.

Peery, A. (2004). *Deep change: Professional development from the inside out.* Lanham, MD: Scarecrow Press.

Pennsylvania Department of Education. (n.d.). Pennsylvania value-added assessment system. *Assessment.* Retrieved May 20, 2008, from http://www.pde.state.pa.us/a_and_t/cwp/view.asp?a=108&Q=108916&a_and_tNav=|6429|&a_and_tNav=|.

Popham, W. J. (2008). *Transformative assessment.* Alexandria, VA: Association for Supervision and Curriculum Development.

Safer, N., & Fleischman, S. (2005). Research matters: How student progress monitoring improves instruction. *Educational Leadership, 62*(5), 81 3.

Schmoker, M. (1996). *Results: The key to continuous school improvement.* Alexandria, VA: Association for Supervision and Curriculum Development.

Scriven, M. S. (1967). The methodology of evaluation. In R. Tyler, R. Gagne, & M. Scriven (Eds.), *AERA monograph review on curriculum evaluation: No. 1* (pp. 39–83). Chicago: Rand McNally.

Snipes, J., Doolittle, F., & Herlihy, C. (2002). *Foundations for success: Case studies of how urban school systems improve student achievement.* New York: MDRC.

Stake, R. (1999). The goods on American education. *Phi Delta Kappan, 80*, 668–672.

Stiggins, R. J. (2002). Assessment crisis: The absence of assessment for learning. *Phi Delta Kappan 83*(10). Retrieved August 1, 2008, from http://electronicportfoios.org/afl/Stiggins-AssessmentCrisis.pdf.

Stecker, P. M., Fuchs, L. S., & Fuchs, D. (2005). Using curriculum-based measurement to improve student achievement: Review of research. *Psychology in the Schools, 42*(8), 795–819.

Stiggins, R. J. (2002). Assessment crisis: The absence of assessment for learning. *Phi Delta Kappan, 83*(10). Retrieved August 1, 2008, from http://electronicportfoios.org/afl/Stiggins-AssessmentCrisis.pdf.

Stronge, J. H. (2007). *Qualities of effective teachers* (2nd ed.). Alexandria, VA: Association for Supervision and Curriculum Development.

Stronge, J. H., & Tucker, P. D. (2000). *Teacher evaluation and student achievement.* Washington, DC: National Education Association.

Stronge, J. H., & Tucker, P. D. (2003). *Handbook on teacher evaluation.* Larchmont, NY: Eye on Education.

Togneri, W., & Anderson, W. E. (2003). *Beyond islands of excellence: What districts can do to improve instruction and achievement in all schools.* Alexandria, VA: Learning Alliance First.

Tomlinson, C. A. (1999). *The differentiated classroom: Responding to the needs of all learners.* Alexandria, VA: Association for Supervision and Curriculum Development.

Tucker, P. D., & Stronge, J. H. (2005). *Linking teacher evaluation and student learning.* Alexandria, VA: Association for Supervision and Curriculum Development.

Tucker, P. D., & Stronge, J. H. (2006). Student achievement and teacher evaluation. In J. H. Stronge (Ed.), *Evaluating teaching: A guide to current thinking and best practice* (2nd ed., pp. 152–167). Thousand Oaks, CA: Corwin Press.

Viadero, D. (2004, January 21). Achievement-gap study emphasizes better use of data. *Education Week, 9.*

Virginia Department of Education, Division of Teacher Education and Licensure. (2000, January). *Guidelines for uniform performance standards and evaluation criteria for teachers, administrators, and superintendents.* Richmond, VA: Author.

Walberg, H. J. (1984). Improving the productivity of America's schools. *Educational Leadership, 41*(8), 19–27.

Webb, L. D., Brigman, G. A., Campbell, C. (2005). Linking school counselors and student success: A replication of the student success skills approach to targeting the academic and social competence of students. *Professional School Counseling, 8*(5), 407–413.

Wharton-McDonald, R., Pressley, M., & Hampston, J. M. (1998). Literacy instruction in nine first-grade classrooms: Teacher characteristics and student achievement. *Elementary School Journal, 99*(2), 101–128.

Wright, S. P., Horn, S. P., & Sanders, W. L. (1997). Teacher and classroom context effects on student achievement: Implications for teacher evaluation. *Journal of Personnel Evaluation in Education, 11,* 57–67.

Yesseldyke, J., & Bolt, D. M. (2007). Effect of technology-enhanced continuous progress monitoring on math achievement. *School Psychology Review, 36*(3), 453–467.

Zila, R. (2005). Thompson School District, personal communication. Reported in P. D. Tucker & J. H. Stronge, *Linking teacher evaluation and student learning* (p. 52). Alexandria, VA: Association for Supervision and Curriculum Development.

Zimmerman, B. J., Bandura, A., & Matinez-Pons, M. (1992). Self-motivation for academic attainment: The role of self-efficacy beliefs and personal goal setting. *American Educational Research Journal, 29*(3), 663–676.